A Treasury of Tennessee Churches

MAYME HART JOHNSON
PHOTOGRAPHS BY DOUG BRACHEY
FOREWORD BY LAMAR ALEXANDER

JM Productions
P.O. BOX 1911 • BRENTWOOD, TN 37027

Photo courtesy Karina McDaniel

A Treasury of
Tennessee Churches

Dedicated to the memory of my parents,
Samuel Henry and Catherine Bowman Hart,
and my husband,
Joseph Samuel Johnson, Jr.

Project Director
Myra M. Ishee
Editorial and Design Staff
John Ishee
Mark Ishee
Rupert Palmer
Typography
P.M. Graphics

0-939298-60-0

State of Tennessee

LAMAR ALEXANDER GOVERNOR

In compiling information for A Treasury of Tennessee Churches, Mayme Hart Johnson adds a valuable contribution to the celebration of Tennessee Homecoming '86 and to the preservation of our state's history.

From Rugby to Bell Buckle to Big Sandy, churches have played a vital role in establishing, nurturing and protecting Tennessee neighborhoods, communities, small towns and large cities. The most important institutions in any community are the churches and the schools.

Mrs. Johnson's own life has been deeply involved in these institutions. She has been a teacher, a home demonstration agent and an historian.

Her collection of photographs and information in this sampling of Tennessee churches is truly a treasure. It is a book that will enrich every family library and that will significantly add to our observance of Homecoming '86.

On behalf of all Tennesseans, I thank her for this book.

Lamar Alexander

Introduction

Tennessee's first settlers built log cabins to live in and log churches to worship in, but long after the log cabins had been supplanted by commodious brick and frame residences they continued to worship in log churches. While a religious people, they saw little need for fine church buildings. Theirs was a preaching religion, not a sacramental religion, and the Word could be preached in the open air, under brush arbors, or in log "meeting houses," as they preferred to call their churches.

The preference for the temporary worship site may have been why the French traveler F. A. Michaux noted in 1802, "There are few churches in Tennessee." The lack of meeting houses of any denomination and the few requirements for worship other than shelter and seating prompted new congregations to use courthouses, Masonic halls, or any space available. In Franklin, the brick Masonic Hall, built in 1828 and the first three-story building in Tennessee, served as the birthplace of many of Williamson County's churches.

The close relationship between the Masonic order and the church in ante-bellum Southern society is manifested in the number of buildings shared by the two institutions. In Cornersville the Methodist congregation shared a handsome Greek Revival building with the Masons, and in Bolivar it was the Presbyterians who shared a fine frame structure with the local lodge. Other instances may be found over the state.

Jonesboro Presbyterian

It was the second generation of Tennesseans, the sons and daughters of the pioneers who had cleared the land and faced the Indians, who began to erect places of worship which were architecturally commensurate with the role which Tennessee was assuming in the nation. Tennessee's own Andrew Jackson was the national hero and the president too! By the 1830's the wealth of the state made available to its citizens most of the luxury goods and cultural advantages found on the Eastern seaboard. The state's educators, preachers, and statesmen were in the forefront of every movement in their respective fields.

In the towns churches became conspicuous not only for their number but for their style, and the rural communities erected churches and meeting houses in keeping with the dignity of their homes. While there were isolated "showplaces" in ante-bellum Tennessee, the domestic architecture was more typically quietly elegant and dignified. It was as if Tennesseans had taken for their guide the rule of the ancient Greeks whose culture they so much admired—"nothing in excess." Beauty depended on line and proportion more than on ornamentation.

Few of the fine churches built in the first half of the nineteenth century in the Federal style have survived. We know them largely through old prints and photographs. The superb Presbyterian church by W. H. Clyde in Jonesboro, built in 1846, retains some Federal characteristics, but like the Jonesboro Methodist Church built at about the same time it is essentially a Greek Revival building.

Masonic Hall, Franklin

St. Mary's Catholic, Nashville

Church of the Holy Trinity, Nashville

It was the Greek Revival style that carried the day in ante-bellum Tennessee in churches as well as residences. The style might vary from the sophistication of Saint Mary's Catholic Church in downtown Nashville, which has long been attributed to William Strickland, to the vernacular approach of local builders throughout the state.

Rural churches of the period, whether of frame or brick, were remarkably similar. Three to four bays in depth with a gabled roof creating pediments at the front and rear elevations in an allusion to classical sources, they were usually entered by two sets of doors. Inside plain pews faced a simple pulpit and that was all. There are examples of beautifully finished interior wainscoting and pulpits, including some which were painted to simulate marble or fine woods.

The Gothic Revival style was favored by the Episcopal Church when that style became popular in the nineteenth century, and the first Episcopal churches in Tennessee were built in that style. The earliest was Saint Paul's in Franklin, which was consecrated in 1835.

The style reached its most correct form in the Church of the Holy Trinity in Nashville, which was designed by Frank Wills of New York City in 1852. Before coming to the United States Wills had practiced in Exeter, England. He was a member of and official architect for the New York Ecclesiastical Society, which believed the church might regain the piety and ethics of the great religious revival of the thirteenth century through a recreation of the architecture and liturgy of the Middle Ages. In 1850 his theories on church architecture had been expressed in a treatise called "Ancient Ecclesiastical Architecture and Its Principles Applied to the Wants of the Church of the Present Day." In this treatise he argued that buildings themselves might be effective teachers of Christian Doctrine.

As with the Greek Revival style, the Gothic style was not always fully understood by local builders, resulting in some vernacular interpretations of great

St. John's Episcopal, Knoxville

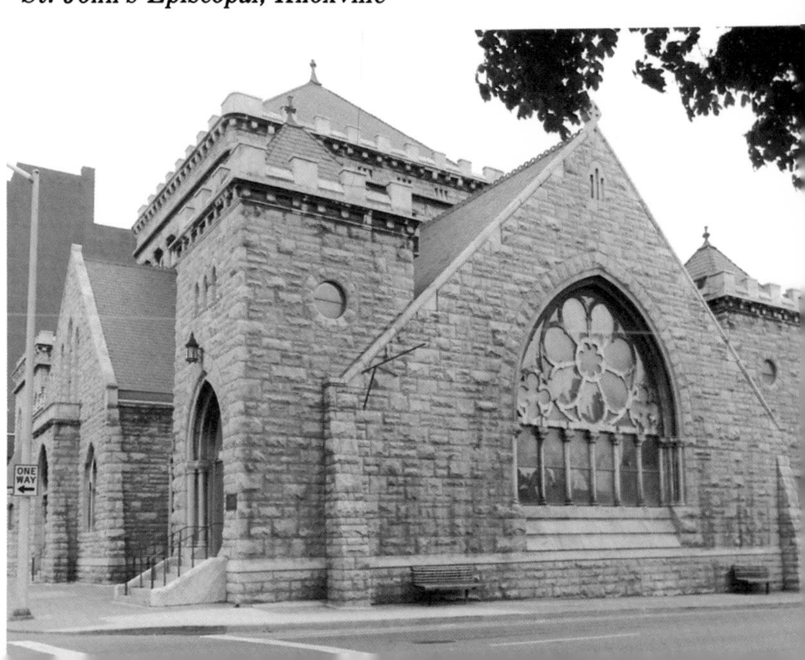

charm. In some instances, such as at the Immanuel Church in La Grange, both styles were happily if naively combined. With the Gothic style came the use of stained glass, the best surviving examples of which are post-Civil War. Several urban churches boast masterpieces of this art, including a number of examples from the studio of Louis Comfort Tiffany.

The post-Civil War period found communities and especially towns replacing worn out or damaged churches with more commodious buildings. These, of which many survive today, reflect the frankly materialistic outlook of the late Victorian era and the more recent aesthetic theories of such writers as John Ruskin. A colorful eclectic configuration of forms running the gamut of architectural vocabulary, these buildings give character to townscapes throughout Tennessee.

The Romanesque style embraced by Henry Hobson Richardson in Boston and the Northeast also found expression in Tennessee, and may be seen to advantage in Saint John's Episcopal Church in Knoxville. In less urban areas vernacular forms of the prevailing styles created hundreds of distinctive church buildings of every denomination. Smaller and simpler than their urban neighbors, they are none the less abundant with style and beauty.

In the period between the two World Wars the Colonial style of church with its sky-reaching spire dominated the church building scene. This form, which derives from the work of Sir Christopher Wren and Thomas Gibbs of seventeenth and eighteenth century England respectively was almost universal in the American Colonies. Its revival in the twentieth century was greatly enhanced by the influence of restored Williamsburg, Virginia on American architecture. As a style it has proved well suited to American Protestantism, combining as it does the rationality of classical thought with Gothic spiritualism. Classical pediments and Gothic spires happily coexist in an architectural form with which any denomination seems comfortable.

Facing the problems of expanding their services and shifting populations, Tennessee churches have until very recently shown little interest in historic preservation. Buildings have been so added to or renovated that in many instances the entire architectural quality of the structure has been lost. Also many architecturally fine church buildings have been abandoned or razed as their memberships opted for more convenient if less compelling structures.

This direction has, however, been changing over the past several years as congregations both large and small, urban and rural have begun to restore their venerated houses of worship and where expansion has been desirable have built architecturally compatible additions.

Tennessee's great treasury of churches is an important resource to which each generation must add rather than deplete. While styles change, the need for churches will remain; as long as there are Tennesseans there will be churches.

First Presbyterian, Jackson

John Kiser, one of the best-known authorities on art and historic architecture in the mid-South, is Professor and Associate Director of the O'More College of Design in Franklin, Tennessee. He also serves on the Governor's Committee to restore the Tennessee State Capitol.

Contents

Publisher's Note

When settlers first crossed the Allegheny Mountains into Tennessee, they changed their location but they didn't change their minds. The spiritual beliefs and practices they brought with them formed the basis for their new way of life in an untamed land. This book, however, is not about spiritual beliefs and practices. Rather, it is about the church buildings erected by various groups—buildings that attest to their frontier faith.

Beginning in the mountains of East Tennessee and spreading to the bluffs of the Mississippi River, churches dot the beautiful Tennessee terrain. The abundance of historic churches in Tennessee makes impossible our desire to include all of them in this book; thus, we have been guided in our selections by three criteria.

First, churches have been selected because of their architecture. The contrast between early wooden structures and modern designs is symbolic of the vast diversity that exists among the people who built them. Many styles of architecture are represented—Gothic, Romanesque, Greek Revival, and even Egyptian Revival. Represented are not only outstanding examples of architectural types but also buildings which do not fit into exact classifications.

Second, consideration was given to the age of the church. Some churches are as old as Tennessee's first settlements because the establishment of a congregation was frequently among the earliest tasks of the settlers. Whenever possible, we have tried to include the oldest example available. Regrettably, very many of the oldest buildings are no longer standing.

Third, attention was given to churches that are associated with significant historical events and people. Paupers and presidents, peacemakers and warriors, famous and infamous—all of these and more found their lives intertwined with churches of the state. This fact lends itself to interesting anecdotal material.

We have also attempted to represent adequately all the major religious groups within Tennessee. Where there was a choice between two equally historic churches, preference was given to the denomination which had fewer entries.

The churches are listed alphabetically by location. Usually a town or city is listed for each church, but a few are listed by county or region, and one is listed under a state park name.

Journey through the state and feel the heartbeat of ancestors who, with faith in God, carved out of the wilderness a lifestyle that provides a legacy for every Tennessean today. Survey the monuments left by these brave pioneers that testify to their faith and determination!

Development of a book of this nature requires many hours of effort by numerous people. We are proud of the result of our efforts and wish to express our appreciation to all the people who helped us. Author Mayme Johnson probably qualifies for sainthood because of her patience with this project. Photographer Doug Brachey was literally re-introduced to Tennessee as he traveled thousands of miles across the state making photographs. Numerous pastors and church members volunteered information about their churches, and their cooperation added immensely to the quality of the book. Our thanks also go to John Kiser for his lucid and interesting Introduction and to Lamar Alexander for his kind words of endorsement in the Foreword. Thanks to all these—and more—who have contributed to the making of a book that is both informative and beautiful.

Saint John's Episcopal, Ashwood

Saint John's Episcopal Church Ashwood

A true example of a plantation church and perhaps the last one built in Tennessee, this church was the fulfillment of the dream of Leonidas Polk, Bishop of the Episcopal Church and General in the Confederate Army. He gave the land, supervised the construction and financially supported this three-year effort.

The other Polk brothers who owned adjoining plantations helped in the building of this church, and there is no mention of outside help being used or sought. Slaves on these plantations cut the trees and hewed the timbers for beams, rafters, and floors. Foundation stones were quarried from a nearby site, and from a large wild cherry tree on the church site the altar, reredos, communion rail and balcony were made.

Polk's mother placed a silver communion service in the church and his sister, Mrs. Kenneth Rayner, gave the marble baptismal font. Both are still used, but the altar silver is kept in Saint Peter's Episcopal Church in Columbia when not in use. The building was completed in 1842 and the bell was placed in the tower in 1849.

"This church is of chaste and simple Gothic architecture...capable of seating...about five hundred people," wrote Leonidas Polk. It measures forty-one by sixty-five feet and the walls are sixteen inches thick, supported by four buttresses on each side.

For the consecration service on September 4, 1842, the church was filled to overflowing. The White families took seats; then the slaves, who had labored on this building for three years, sat in every available space right up to the edge of the altar. They were joined by their families.

Several members of the Polk family are buried in the cemetery under the magnolia trees at the rear of the church. Also buried there is Bishop Otey, founder of the Episcopal Church in Tennessee and onetime rector of Saint John's, and all but one of the deceased Bishops of Tennessee. Although Leonidas Polk wished to be buried here, he was killed at the battle of Pine Mountain in 1864 and buried in the crypt beneath the chancel of Saint Paul's Episcopal Church in Augusta, Georgia. In 1945 his remains were removed to Christ Church Cathedral in New Orleans.

On September 7, 1870, Saint John's Church enjoyed its largest and most fashionable wedding. Margaret Ann Pillow, daughter of Confederate General Gideon Pillow, married Daniel Fount Wade, former Captain of the "Bigby Grays" of the Third Tennessee Infantry. Records of the day state that "miles of buggies" headed for Saint John's, and "not a single conveyance was left in the livery stables in Columbia." Then, "under an arch of magnolia leaves the couple repeated their vows encircled by fourteen attendants," all lovely, charming ladies together with groomsmen who had served in the Confederate army.

Today, the only church service held is the annual Whitsunday service. The Scottish Rite Masons hold sunrise services on Easter morning.

First Baptist Church
Athens

First Baptist Church of Athens was organized on July 24, 1824, with eleven members. They worshipped in private homes for a time and later built a log house at Cedar Grove Cemetery. There are few records of this church for nearly forty years,

First Baptist, Athens

and it ceased to exist for a few years. In 1871, the church was reorganized at a meeting held in the McMinn County courthouse with twelve members.

In 1887 a building committee was formed to raise money and make preparation for erecting a sanctuary. The new church was dedicated in 1890, and Reverend J.T. Barrow became the first pastor in that building.

In 1926, with the Reverend H.A. Todd as pastor, First Baptist Church of Athens undertook the task of building a building for Sunday School in the Morningside Community. The Women's Missionary Union of the Athens Church, organized in 1889, raised most of the money for that building.

On August 10, 1941, the first worship service was held in a new sanctuary. This building was soon outgrown, and in January 1964, plans for another sanctuary were made. The first service in this Greek Revival church was held March 26, 1967.

Mars Hill Presbyterian Church
Athens

On November 2, 1823, four years after the Cherokee Indians had ceded the land to the United States government and forty days after Athens had become the county seat of McMinn County, the Reverend William Eagleton, pastor of the Presbyterian Church in Kingston, organized Mars Hill Presbyterian Church in Athens.

Mars Hill Presbyterian, Athens

The original Presbyterian sanctuary was a small temporary one near the First Baptist Church. In March 1837 a building committee was appointed and a new site was purchased; a brick building which served as both church and civic meeting house was completed in 1838. Pews were sold and rented.

In March 1834, records show that the first of a series of indictments of members for moral offenses began. Punishments were meted out for profanity, sending girls to dancing school, and general un-Christian behavior. Some members were suspended for various periods of time and others were excommunicated.

Reverend George A. Caldwell became pastor in 1852, but left in 1863 to become a chaplain in the Confederate Army. Stresses of the times are not mentioned in minutes of the Sessions from 1857 to 1863, although there had occurred a distinct rift in this church over abolition of slavery.

The Union army arrived in Athens in the late summer of 1863 and many citizens, including Reverend Caldwell, fled south, while others were interned by the Union army for the duration. Church records for 1863 show this notation on a fly leaf of Volume II: "George A. Caldwell, former pastor of this church, is now a renegade and belongs to the rebel army. Trying to instill some principal of religion into the minds of the rebel soldiery. Alas, a vain attempt. Quid est."

The war years saw Mars Hill Church without a pastor most of the time. When hostilies ceased, the church building was in bad repair. Renovation and restoration were attempted, but the work was slow. Worship was held in McKeldin's Hall on the corner of Jackson and Washington Streets during that time. In 1878 the shattered walls and debris were removed and the church was rebuilt.

On the night of January 12, 1944, a fire was discovered in the building. Extensive damage was done to the interior, particularly the chancel area. The organ and antique altar furniture and appointments were destroyed. Valuable stained glass windows were damaged, but were later restored. Extensive renovations and building additions were completed in 1960.

Bell Buckle United Methodist Church
Bell Buckle

As early as 1807, the Duck River Circuit included a congregation on Bell Buckle Creek known as Salem Methodist Church and Campground. Tradition says that in 1807 neighbors cut round poles and erected a meeting house on land belonging to Mr. Norvell and called it Salem.

Reverend John B. McFerrin stated that the meeting house was made of logs and poles covered with clapboards held in place by weight poles. This small structure was soon outgrown, and Norvell's Camp Ground was established.

A hewn log church replaced the original, and the Annual Conference met in that building in 1821. A frame structure later replaced that log house. In 1875 a brick sanctuary was erected in Bell Buckle.

Webb School for Boys moved from Culleoka to Bell Buckle in 1886. Sawney Webb, owner and headmaster of the school, was a devout Methodist, and soon a close relationship between the Methodist church and Webb School developed.

The present Gothic building was completed in 1893. Many descendants of original Salem members worship here still.

Bell Buckle United Methodist

Mount Zion Baptist, Big Sandy

Mount Zion Baptist Church
Big Sandy

This simple log building between the Big Sandy and Tennessee Rivers was built in 1893 on the site of an earlier church built in 1852. Minutes of the Western District Baptist Association show that two delegates from Mount Zion were in attendance, and that the church had twenty-four members.

In 1943 the Tennessee Valley Authority bought the church property, consisting of 2.7 acres. The congregation disbanded and an agreement was made allowing use of the building and grounds for an annual homecoming picnic on the first Sunday in July. The Reverend D.W. Billington was the last pastor of Mount Zion Church.

About fifty yards northeast of the church can be seen a roadway over which Nathan Bedford Forrest traveled with his men on October 31 and November 1, 1864, in the Johnsonville Expedition to Pilot Knob during the Civil War.

Acuff Chapel
Blountville

This small church constructed of hand-hewn logs is believed to have been built as early as 1784 on land belonging to Timothy Acuff. Micajah Adams, a Revolutionary War veteran who lived nearby, is said to have assisted Acuff in building this chapel. A very old cemetery in which Timothy Acuff and Micajah Adams are buried is adjacent to the churchyard. The building has served as a place of worship for a Methodist congregation and as a school for neighborhood children.

Bishop Asbury preached here many times and was the guest of the Acuff family. The building outlived its purpose as a house of worship, was sold, moved, covered with boards, and used as a dwelling house for many years.

About 1960, the Holston Conference purchased the chapel, removed it to the original site, and restored it to its early appearance with chimney, fireplace, and board roof. It is now a shrine of American Methodism.

Acuff Chapel, Blountville

Blountville Presbyterian Church
Blountville

This church was organized in the home of Samuel Rhea in 1820. The first building stood on Graveyard Hill on the western side of the village. Reverend Andrew Campbell became the first pastor in December of 1821.

The present Greek Revival building is the fourth one. The cornerstone was laid in 1935.

On July 27, 1836, during a sermon in the Graveyard Hill Church by Reverend Daniel Rogan, President Andrew Jackson, A. J. Donaldson, Colonel McClellan, and fifteen other men arrived at the church. Reverend Rogan paused to recognize the President and then finished his sermon. At its close, he introduced the visitors to the congregation.

Blountville Presbyterian

Rockhold Methodist Church and Campground
Bluff City

Amid giant oak trees on the south bank of the Holston River stands Rockhold Methodist Church and Campground, which dates from 1816. It was part of the plantation of William Rockhold, who donated it to the Methodist Episcopal Church, South in 1853. The Rockhold family arrived in Sullivan County in 1795, and its members were prominent in public as well as religious life. There is a spring on the one and a half acre tract.

The architectural style of the church is of German origin and is referred to as "western tower" design. There are two towers, one of which is crowned by a tall spire.

aint James Episopal Church
olivar

he Reverend James H. Otey organized this church vith thirty members on April 17, 1834. The group vorshipped in the Hardeman County courthouse for nany years.

On July 27, 1840, a lot was purchased for $175 at he corner of Lafayette and Washington Streets. At cost of $375, a brick church measuring 32 by 44 eet was constructed and consecrated in 1845.

Reverend William Crane Gray, pastor of the hurch in 1860, left to serve as a chaplain in the onfederate army. After the war, he served Saint ames again until 1881, and later became Bishop of lorida.

When the Civil War had ended and the church vas left in a bad state of repair, it was decided that new church was needed. In 1869, additional land vas purchased and a contract made with Willis and loan for the building of the new church. The rchitect for the 48 by 70 foot church was Mr. letcher Sloan, who designed several southern hurches and courthouses as well as many of the lder buildings on the University of Alabama ampus.

Several memorial windows grace this Gothic hurch. Of special interest is the window for General tho French Strahl and Lieutenant John Henry Iarsh. Bishop Quintard related in his memoirs: "Just efore moving toward Franklin, General Strahl came o me and said, 'I want to make you a present' and resented me with a splendid horse named Lady olk. I used the horse through the remainder of the var and at its close sold her and with the money rected in Saint James Church, Bolivar, a memorial vindow to General Strahl and his adjutant, ieutenant John H. Marsh. Both of these men I had aptized but a few months previously, and both were onfirmed by Bishop Elliott."

Rockhold Methodist Church and Campground (above)

Saint James Episcopal, Bolivar (below)

First Baptist Church
Bolivar

Organized in 1835, First Baptist Church worshipped in homes or the courthouse for several months. The first pastor and organizer of this church was Levin Savage. The first deed for church property is dated March 1837, and a frame church with a slave gallery was built here. Federal troops seized this building, used it for several purposes, and burned it down when they left.

The Methodist church allowed the Baptist congregation to worship in their building for a time, and in April 1866 the Baptists reorganized and built another frame church, which was used until 1897 when it was sold. A brick sanctuary was constructed on Warren Street in 1898, and a new church was erected in 1922.

The present church, a Victorian adaptation of Gothic Revival architecture, was dedicated in 1961 with Dr. R.G. Lee of Memphis delivering the dedication sermon.

A three manual organ, one of the largest in this part of the state, was installed in 1966. A bell which hung in the old church is still in use in this one. It was cast in Louisville, Kentucky, in 1868, and members contributed brass andirons, knives, spoons, and gold rings for it.

Bolivar Presbyterian

First Baptist, Bolivar

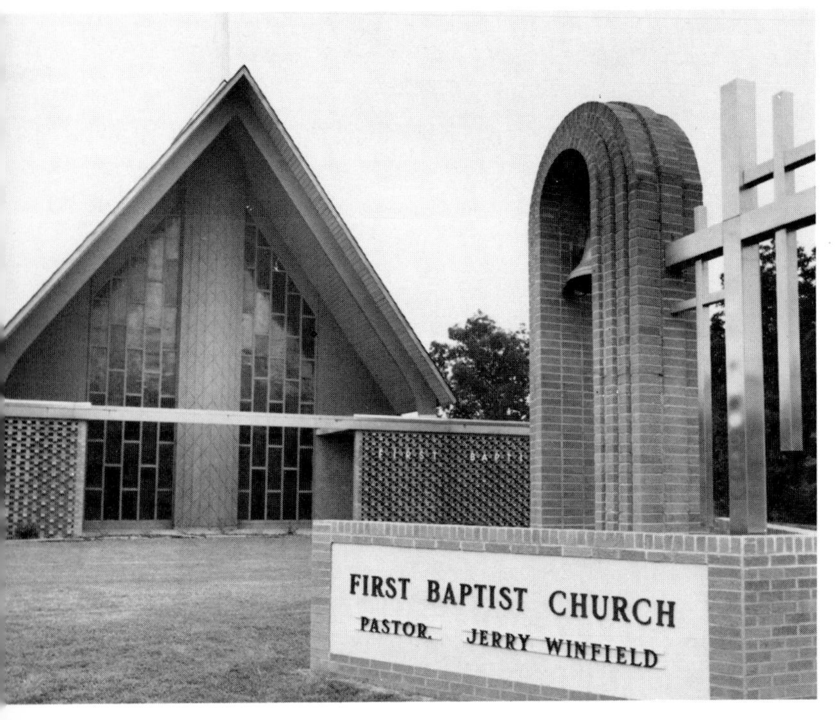

Bolivar Presbyterian Church
Bolivar

Bolivar Presbyterian Church was founded on November 12, 1852, with twenty charter members. The last surviving charter member was Louisa Neely Coleman, who died in 1938 at age 102. Members of her family are still active in the church.

The original Greek Revival building is still in use, and is the oldest brick church in Hardeman County. Built in 1853, it housed the sanctuary on the first floor and the Masonic Lodge upstairs. Restoration was necessary to the rear of the building in 1982 after a portion of it collapsed.

During the Civil War, General Lew Wallace, author of *Ben Hur*, and his Union soldiers were stationed near the church and worshipped here at times.

The first Bible used here is dated 1853 and is now displayed on a lectern. The pulpit furniture and rare inner blinds are original to the church. The pipe organ, given in 1882 by Judge and Mrs. James Fentress, was originally pumped by hand.

wen's Chapel Church of Christ
rentwood

The meeting house" of Owen's Chapel Church was uilt in 1859 on land donated by Jim C. Owen, who as baptized by James A. Harding, co-founder with avid Lipscomb of David Lipscomb College in ashville.

Constructed of brick made on the site, Owen's hapel still has its original tongue-and-groove tin oof, imported from England, and orginal pews and ulpit. The two front doors and partition down the enter of the church separating the pews, and nerefore men and women in the sanctuary, were ypical features of early churches.

Forty by seventy feet with a high ceiling, the nterior of the church was heated by pot-bellied toves until coal heaters replaced them. Gas heating eplaced coal heaters in 1950. Candles lighted the hurch until 1870 when oil lamps came into fashion, nly to be replaced by electrictity in 1929.

Construction continued during the Civil War. The ld leatherbound record states that the congregation as failed to meet only three times since 1859; on ne occasion, "the Yankees were foraging," and on nother "a near cloudburst" interfered.

The first organizational sermon was preached by Colbert Fanning, who founded the girls' school by hat name. David Lipscomb, E.G. Sewell, founder of he Gospel Advocate in Nashville, William Lipscomb, Granville Lipscomb, F.C. Sowell, Jr., J.A. Harding, nd J.C. McQuiddy, founder of McQuiddy Printing Company, are a few of the early preachers here.

The ministries of Owen's Chapel include support of nissionaries, orphans and widows, college students, new churches, food and clothing for the poor, and sometimes money for coffins. In the 1870's and 1880's considerable preaching was done among the Indians, and at the present time, the offering on all fifth Sundays is given to the Tennessee Orphan's Home in Spring Hill, Tennessee.

Owen's Chapel Church of Christ, Brentwood

Liberty United Methodist, Brentwood

Liberty United Methodist Church
Brentwood

Colonel Green Hill, a Methodist minister and a former Revolutionary War Officer, and his wife moved into the Brentwood area in 1799. Soon they started a Methodist congregation, and a small building for worship was built in 1807 which he named "Liberty Hill Methodist Church." He preached here for many years.

Records show that the Western Conference of the Methodist Church held its first conference at Liberty Hill in 1808. According to Dr. James Reed Cox, United Methodist Church Historian, "Col. and Mrs. Hill kept seventy preachers from seven states in their home for a week" during that first meeting of the Conference.

The Conference was on the verge of closing Liberty Hill Church in 1970, but Dr. Cox, assisted by loyal members of the congregation, succeeded in having the Commission on Archives and History take charge of the church and to continue regular worship. The cemetery in which the Hill family is buried has been designated a Methodist Shrine.

Christ Church Episcopal, Brownsville

Brick Church Presbyterian Church
Brick Church

This vernacular Greek Revival Church is a white wood clapboard building. The original church here was a brick one, and the rural neighborhood took its name from the church.

Brick Church was founded in 1840 by the Reverend Edward McMillan with Robert Gordon, Sr., and his wife, Martin Lane and his wife, John N. Shields, Eleanor McLure, and Mary A. McMillan.

The interior features yellow poplar wainscoating and doors, the original pulpit, and black walnut Victorian Renaissance chairs with leather upholstered seats on the rostrum. Outside there is an entablature all around, with a pediment front and back. Twelve over twelve windows are on both sides, and one small stained glass window is placed behind the altar. An ancient privy still stands at the back, and a cemetery surrounds the church.

Brick Church Presbyterian

Christ Church Episcopal
Brownsville

When Reverend Thomas Wright and Reverend John Chilton traveled to West Tennessee from Salisbury, North Carolina, they each kept a record of their journey and the events which followed. Wright recorded that he and Chilton organized an Episcopal congregation called Zion Church in Brownsville on August 25, 1832, with five communicants present.

The Reverend John Chilton, first rector of Zion Church, was also the first Episcopal minister to be ordained in Tennessee. The name of the church was changed to Christ Church in 1898 by consent of Bishop Gailor.

Worship was held in an upper room in the courthouse for many years. The Gothic church still in use was erected in 1846, when the list of communicants had grown to twelve.

Miss Minna Wendel served as organist for many years and is remembered by many as "the most faithful member Christ Church ever had." She lived close to ninety years and was first diocesan president of the Daughters of the King in Tennessee.

Temple Adas Israel, Brownsville

Temple Adas Israel
Brownsville

Sometime after 1860, Joe Sternberg immigrated from Germany and settled in Brownsville. He brought a century-old Torah, which became the foundation for a Jewish community and house of worship in this rural West Tennessee county.

The Adas Israel congregation was organized when Jacob and Karoline Felsenthal offered a room in their home as a place for the Torah in 1867. The Anker and Rothschild families provided places for worship in their homes and businesses and kept the Torah in their homes at times.

A Reformed Jewish congregation built and dedicated their Temple in 1882 but has never had a resident rabbi. The congregation has remained small.

Saint Michael's Catholic, Cedar Hill

Saint Michael's Catholic Church
Cedar Hill

Saint Michael's, established May 8, 1842, is the oldest active Catholic church in Tennessee; Saint Michael's Male and Female Academy, opened in 1846, is one of the oldest boarding academies in the state. The school has been staffed by clerics since the beginning.

Preserved here are crude candle snuffers and iron bread makers and cutters dating to 1842. An altar Missal, original in the church, was printed in 1762 at Plantin Press in Antwerp, Belgium, and brought to Saint Michael's by Gustave Bouchard, a Frenchman who taught in the Academy. Early altar cards are also preserved at the church.

A statue of the Blessed Mother, placed here in 1895, was bought with money raised by young people's groups, who published and sold twenty monthly handwritten magazines.

Father Abram Ryan, poet-priest of the Confederacy, served as Missioner here in 1864-65.

Charleston Cumberland Presbyterian Church
Charleston

This Greek Revival building is a fine example of rural church architecture in southeastern Tennessee. It stands in a walled cemetery amid monuments from many periods. The church was organized and the building erected in 1860, in the first white settlement in Bradley County and one of the earliest in this part of Tennessee.

As early as 1819, Charleston was a trading post in the Ocoee District—seventeen years before Bradley County was chartered in 1836.

Charleston Cumberland Presbyterian Church was founded a short time before the outbreak of the Civil War. The first pastor was Reverend Hiram Douglas, leader in the Cumberland Presbyterian Church and Moderator of the General Assembly in 1865, the highest honor of the denomination.

The church was held by the Union army and used for many purposes during the war. It was fifty years later that the United States government paid the congregation $424 for damages done to the building.

Charleston Cumberland Presbyterian

Charlotte Cumberland Presbyterian Church
Charlotte

Charlotte Cumberland Presbyterian Church has stood as a historical landmark in Charlotte and Dickson County since Reverends Finis Ewing, Samuel King, and Ephraim McLean met in the home of Reverend Samuel McAdow, eight miles south of Charlotte, on February 3, 1810, and there laid the groundwork for the founding of this church.

It was 1820 before any house of worship was erected, and Reformed Presbyterians, Methodists, and perhaps Baptists had already built churches in Charlotte. In December 1837, forty men and women organized the Cumberland Presbyterian Church in Charlotte. Contributions came slowly, and the Depression of 1837 had its effect on this once flourishing village.

More than a decade had passed when three generous and determined men—Leonard Lane Beech, Benjamin Corlew, and Clark Larkins—contributed funds for building the church. Bricks were made and fired within the town limits at a kiln owned by James Dickson, and the slaves of Beech and Corlew provided the labor and carpentry skills.

In November 1863, two Federal regiments numbering four hundred men occupied Charlotte, and the village became known as "Camp Charlotte." The Cumberland Presbyterian Church became a hospital and sustained much damage. Members and friends were able to repair the damage, and in 1905 the Federal government made partial restitution. Additional funds have been donated over the years, and today Charlotte Cumberland Presbyterian Church is unique in quality and appearace among rural and small town churches in Tennessee.

A bell with deep low tones cast in Pittsburgh, Pennsylvania in 1845, hangs in the belfry and can be heard for great distances. It was used on a steamboat which plied the waters of both the Cumberland and Harpeth Rivers, and is said to have been taken from the burning boat and given to the church.

Charlotte Cumberland Presbyterian

First Baptist Church (Gateway Avenue) Chattanooga

Chattanooga Baptist Church was formed in 1840 as a mission of First Baptist Church in Nashville. When the city of Chattanooga was laid out, each existing church received a lot, but no church group in the city was financially able to build a house of worship at that time. "Union House," a log building on Walnut Street, was used by all denominations on alternate Sundays.

Dr. Matthew Hillsman, who had nurtured the fledgling Baptist church, left in 1843 to become President of Mossy Creek (later Carson-Newman) College, and in that year both Baptists and Methodists moved into a log house at Fifth and Lookout Streets. A frame building was built on the same site and named Chattanooga Baptist Church.

In September 1863, the Union Army occupied Chattanooga, and the Baptist Church became a hospital. After hostilities ceased, the church became a Post Chapel and was badly damaged.

Church leader Foley Vaughn sought out the scattered members and mortgaged his home to help repair the building. The ladies of First Baptist Church in Charleston, South Carolina, donated a handsome communion service to the church: a pitcher, a chalice and some plates from the set are prized possessions now.

In 1887, it was decided to build a new church on the same site. The existing building was donated to a group of members who chose to form another church, which they named Central Baptist. The building was put on logs, rolled down Georgia Avenue by way of McCallie, and placed on the southwest corner of Palmetto Street.

Sometime in 1900, the pastor, Dr. Broughes, announced that he would deliver a sermon on "Sin." The crowd was so large that the pastor could not enter the building. Fearing a fire and loss of life, he called the fire department on Georgia Avenue to bring fire-fighting equipment and stand by. When the engines, hook, and ladder arrived, he had the firemen place the ladder against a wall. He then climbed the ladder to a second story window, which he opened and delivered his sermon on "Sin."

In 1956, the funeral service for Senator Estes Kefauver, whose great-grandfather, Reverend J.P. Kefauver, had served as pastor of this church, was held here.

A magnificent new church of Neo-Classical design was dedicated in 1967. It features a two hundred foot tall tower and a bronze bell cast by C.L. Hawks in Cincinnati.

First Baptist (Gateway Avenue), Chattanooga

First Baptist Church (Eighth Street) Chattanooga

This church is not only one of the earliest Black congregations but also one of the oldest buildings in the city. An army chaplain named Van Horne organized Shiloh Baptist in 1866 with a group of former slaves. They worked for thirty years to raise enough money to purchase land and materials, and then built their church with their own hands. This church stands as a tower of religious, social, and cultural strength and importance for the Black population which it serves.

The first worship services were held in homes of members until a new building referred to as "Old Temporary" was built at the corner of Tenth and Lindsey Streets. "Old Temporary" burned and was replaced with another building on the same site. It was during the pastorate of G.D. Olden in 1888-91 that the present building was begun.

Twice this congregation has divided, and three other churches have resulted from these divisions—St. James Church, Shiloh First Church, and New Monumental Church. Finally the name of the original church was changed from Shiloh to First Baptist.

The Gothic Revival building retains its basic original appearance, although some alterations have been made.

First Baptist (Eighth Street), Chattanooga

Saints Peter and Paul Catholic Church Chattanooga

The church stands on a high hill in the downtown area and is the home of the first permanent Catholic congregation in Chattanooga. Built in 1857, it was for many years the only Catholic Church in the Chattanooga area.

The area around the 1857 church was called "Irish Hill" because the first resident priest in this isolated area, Father Brown, bought a large tract of land here and sold it to members of the congregation at cost.

A new church was begun in 1860, but work was interrupted by the Civil War, as building stones were seized by Federal troops. When the government made partial payment of damages in 1888, construction was resumed. Dedicated in 1890, this Gothic church was designed by Michigan architect Peter Dedericks, Jr.

Notable features of the interior include a groined vault ceiling, handsome Stations of the Cross, and a series of fourteen stained glass windows dedicated to Saint Peter and Saint Paul. The windows were installed in 1890, and each measures six by thirty feet. Those on the southeast side depict events in the life of Peter, and those on the northwest depict events in the life of Paul.

Saints Peter and Paul Catholic, Chattanooga

Mizpah Congregation, Chattanooga

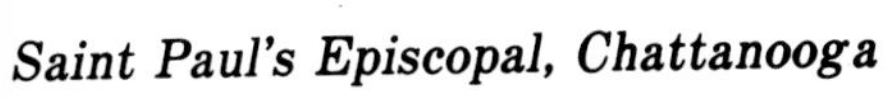

Saint Paul's Episcopal, Chattanooga

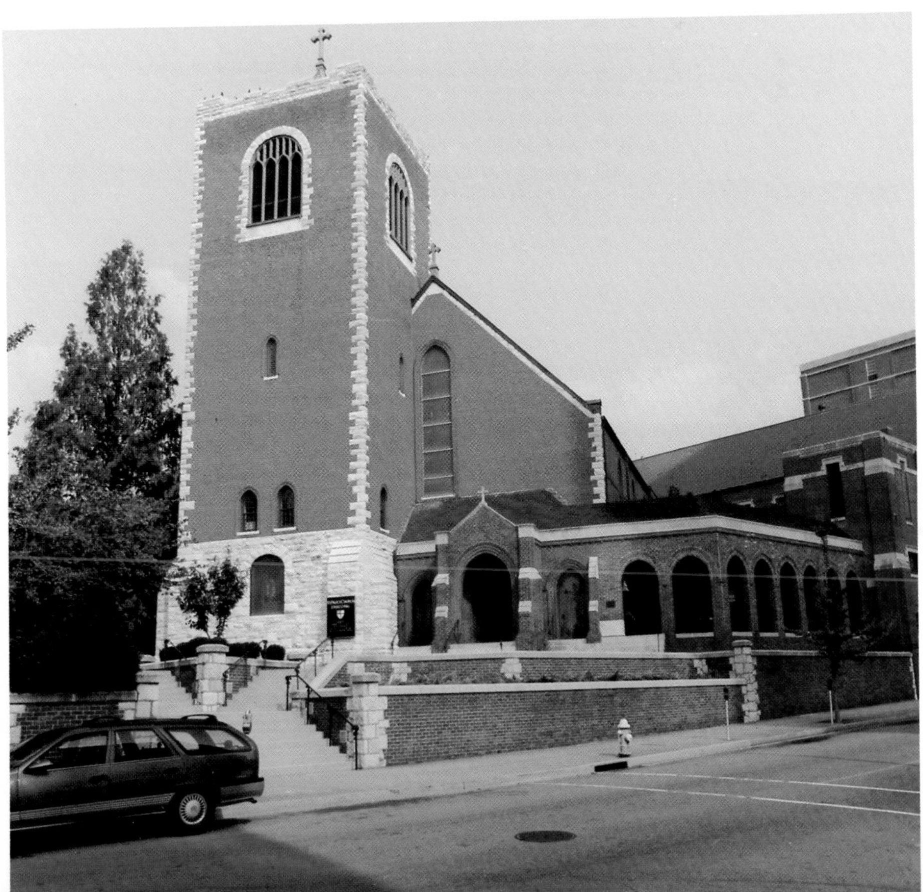

Mizpah Congregation
Chattanooga

On May 20, 1866, twenty-one young Jewish men met in Chattanooga and formed a society called Chebra Gamilar Chaced. The next year the name was changed to Hebrew Benevolent Association. Meetings were held in the home of Jacob Bach, who served as lay-rabbi, *chazen*, and *schochet*. Six churches were active in the town at the time.

In 1866, land which had served as a potter's field was acquired for a cemetery. It is the place of the Jewish cemetery at the present time.

An epidemic of yellow fever spread across Chattanooga in 1878 and claimed three hundred and sixty-six lives, among them Miss Hattie Ackerman. She was a teacher who remained in the city to nurse the sick and has been cited in Chattanooga history for heroism during the epidemic. She lies in Mizpah Cemetery. Mr. Julius Ochs, who moved to Chattanooga from Knoxville in 1878, is remembered for his generosity of time and talents to that cemetery.

Activities moved to Concordia Hall on Market Street and property at 429 Walnut Street was purchased. A new house of worship was dedicated September 4, 1894.

In July 1902, plans were initiated for building a new Temple at the corner of Oak and Lindsey Streets, and by 1922 Rabbi Holsberg began planning for another building. The property at Oak and Lindsey Streets and land at 923 McCallie Avenue was acquired. On March 17, 1927, ground was broken and three months later a cornerstone was laid. On March 23, 1928, the Julius and Bertha Ochs Memorial Temple was dedicated.

In May 1959, the old building was demolished and construction on the present Temple was commenced. It was dedicated February 19, 1960.

Saint Paul's Episcopal Church
Chattanooga

Saint Paul's Parish is the "mother church" of all parishes in the Chattanooga area. Four of its rectors have gone on to become bishops, including John VanderHorst, who became Bishop of Tennessee. Saint Paul's has a long and interesting history, which is detailed by Dr. E.S. Lindsey in his two-volume *Centennial History: Saint Paul's Episcopal Church.*

When Saint Paul's Parish was first organized, Chattanooga had a total population of less than 2,500. Colonel James Anderson Whiteside came to Chattanooga from Kentucky in 1838, and on January 17, 1853, he founded this church in his home.

On Sunday, June 1, 1852, Bishop James Hervey Otey held the first recorded church service in Chattanooga on the second floor of a warehouse (later the armory) at Market and Fourth streets. Reverend John Sandals, first rector of Saint Paul's, was sent as a missionary to the Chattanooga area soon after, and on January 1, 1853, he held service in the same "upper room" where Bishop Otey had worshipped.

In 1858 the decision was made to build a new brick church with a seating capacity of 300. Many problems arose while the church was being built, including the intervention of the Civil War, during which the church house was used as a hospital and warehouse. Finally the new church was finished, but by 1885 the membership had exceeded the new building's capacity and another building project was begun.

Reverend George Dumbell, D.D., originally from the Isle of Man and a Cambridge graduate, was installed as rector of Saint Paul's on January 1, 1885. During his term Saint Paul's current structure was planned and built.

Plans for the new church house, rectory, and parish house were drawn by architect W. Halsey Wood, another native of the Isle of Man. Wood had designed the Cathedral of Saint John the Divine in New York City, as well as the Chapel at Sewanee and Saint Mary's in Memphis. He drew inspiration from an old abbey on the Isle of Man in planning Saint Paul's; the church's brick interior is of Venetian Gothic style. Wood died before Saint Paul's was completed.

Many gifts were received toward the new church, including $250 from Commodore Cornelius Vanderbilt and $100 from William McAdoo, Woodrow Wilson's son-in-law.

The cornerstone of the current building was laid on September 7, 1886, by Bishop Quintard. The first service in the new location was held on May 10, 1888, but the old church was still used until July 22 of that year, after which it was abandoned completely.

Among the distinctive features of Saint Paul's is the altar, which is made of Italian marble and features hand-painted artwork with the figure of Christ in the center and pictures of children on either side. The altar was donated by Mrs. William Yonge in memory of her husband, who had been the primary fundraiser for the new church and who died of typhoid fever before its completion.

Saint Paul's was consecrated in 1901 when the building debt was removed. On September 7, 1986, Saint Paul's will celebrate the 100th birthday of the current building, and will also install its eighteenth rector this year.

Red Bank Baptist Church
Chattanooga

In a history of Red Bank community, Walter Wood stated that the first settlers were Methodists and Cumberland Presbyterians. No records of early churches exist, but a log church building is known to have stood on what is now Morrison Springs Road.

In 1870, the people in the area agreed to build a Union church, and Alfred Rogers donated one acre of land for the church site. A one-room building was constructed, and Methodists, Baptists and Cumberland Presbyterians, worshipping on alternating Sundays, met here until October 1923, when the congregations decided to build their own places of worship.

The Baptist group completed their first church on Ashland Terrace in May 1925. It had been organized with seven members and Reverend A.P. Gallaher as pastor, and was called Pleasant Hill Church.

The present sanctuary was completed in 1958. This Georgian Colonial church of red brick with Indiana limestone trim has a steeple 162 feet high. Pews and pulpit furnishings are white enameled maple with mahogany trim. A three manual Moller pipe organ was installed in 1959.

Red Bank Baptist, Chattanooga

Trinity Episcopal Church
Clarksville

This Romanesque Revival style stone building was copied from a church in Kent, England, and is considered one of the finest houses of worship in Tennessee.

After worshipping in the Masonic Hall in Clarksville for two years, the small Episcopal congregation began construction of a church in 1834. When the building was near completion, however, it was declared structurally unsafe. Razed and rebuilt, it was consecrated June 23, 1838.

From 1864 to 1874, the rector of Trinity Church was Reverend Samuel Ringgold, who established several mission Sunday Schools in the area and who later led a revival of the Episcopal Church in East Tennessee. An incident indicating his conciliatory spirit after the war is recorded by Robert E. Wood, a later rector of the church, in a letter to the *Clarksville Leaf-Chronicle*.

On the Easter Sunday following President Lincoln's assassination on Good Friday, the traditional red and white flowers were displayed in the church; Dr. Mary Walker, the U. S. Army's first woman surgeon, came to morning services and believed the flowers to be Confederate colors, in celebration of Lincoln's death. That evening she returned with many Union soldiers.

Advised to cancel the service, Ringgold instead asked for an hour's delay. He then "went to his home and gathered up the letters he had received from families to whom he had ministered on both sides. He returned to the church and preached on peace, quoting from these letters of heartache and suffering among fellow human beings divided in war." The effect of his sermon was such that Dr. Walker placed a small American flag in the offering, which Ringgold accepted as "her gift to God."

Soon after the war, the 1838 church showed signs of deterioration, and in 1875 it was demolished. On June 30, 1875, the cornerstone of the present building was laid; the new church was consecrated in 1881. Gray-tinted blue limestone was used in the construction under the direction of Mr. Andreworth as architect and John Conroy as contractor.

Trinity Episcopal, Clarksville

**Madison Street United Methodist Church
Clarksville**

This cathedral-like church is the third built by this congregation. The first, erected in 1831, was located at the corner of Main and Fourth Streets, and was later sold to the Cumberland Presbyterian Church. A larger building was erected at Franklin and Fifth Streets in 1842.

In 1882, the cornerstone was laid for the present church. The building was completed in early 1883 at a cost of $40,000; C.G. Rosenplanter was the architect.

Two steeples grace the front of this church; one contains a thousand-pound bell, which had hung in the church on Franklin Street since 1854 and was moved here in 1883. The bell was cracked in 1935 and recast in 1940.

The Madison Street Church is noted for its beautiful stained glass, of which the oculus window in the facade is particularly striking. The beamwork which supports the roof was constructed by the Pittsburgh Bridge Company; the Jardine pipe organ was installed in 1893 at a cost of $3,000.

According to tradition, the original plans for this church were scaled for a smaller building than was required, and some structural elements purchased were unsuitable; these were donated to St. Peter's A. M. E. church, whose roof support system is today very similar to that of Madison Street Methodist.

This building was placed on the National Register of Historic Sites and Places in 1976.

First Presbyterian Church
Clarksville

At a meeting conducted by the Reverend Lyman Whitney, a missionary from Connecticut, a Presbyterian congregation was organized on May 22, 1822, in Clarksville. The Montgomery County Courthouse and the Masonic Hall served as meeting places for this group until 1840, when their first church was erected on the corner of Main and Third Streets.

On May 19, 1876, the cornerstone was laid for the present church on the same location. It was dedicated on May 26, 1878.

Pews from the former church and additional matching pews were installed. A bell weighing 2,790 pounds was placed in one of the steeples. An unusual water-powered organ, designed by Dr. J.W. Caldwell, the organist, was also installed. It was soon converted to a bellows system because when the water power was used it reduced water pressure in the whole neighborhood. The organ was later converted to electricity.

The church was placed on the National Register of Historic Sites and Places in 1976.

Madison Street United Methodist, Clarksville

First Presbyterian, Clarksville

Saint Luke's Episcopal, Cleveland

Broad Street Methodist, Cleveland

Broad Street United Methodist Church
Cleveland

The oldest portion of Broad Street Church was built in 1893 of red brick; it houses the sanctuary and has a square three-storied tower. A religious school building constructed in 1922 is attached to the west side of the church.

The east facade of this Victorian Romanesque church features two towers with pyramid roofs, cresting and finials, arched entrances and cornices. The overall building design is in the shape of a Greek cross, with gable roof structure, dentiled cornices, and louvered vents.

The ceiling in the sanctuary, featuring hammerbeam truss work emanating from hexagonal pilasters at the corners of the cross vault, is unique in this section of southeastern Tennessee. Stained glass windows displaying religious motifs in Art Nouveau style provide a pleasant background for the dark wooden pews, altar, and cabinet work in the sanctuary.

Saint Luke's Episcopal Church
Cleveland

This cruciform building of Victorian Gothic architecture was designed and built in 1873 by Peter J. Williamson, who also designed the Synagogue in Nashville, Central State Hospital, buildings in McMinnville, and buildings on Vanderbilt University campus. This church was one of his finest buildings.

With a square three-storied tower, arched lancet windows and doors, brick buttresses, and broad gabled roof, this handsome church is virtually unchanged from its original appearance and condition. The church, parish house and Gothic marble mausoleum occupy an entire block in downtown Cleveland, surrounded by a crenelated stone wall with iron gates.

Saint Luke's church was the gift of John H. Craigmiles of Cleveland in memory of his seven year old daughter, Nina, who was killed in a railroad accident on Saint Luke's Day in 1871.

First United Methodist Church
Columbia

Construction on First Methodist Church was begun in March 1876 by Anthony Gholson, and the cornerstone was laid in April. W. K. Dodson was the architect.

The cornerstone ceremony was an important event in Columbia, with the entire town taking part. A procession led by the Columbia Helicon Silver Band, followed by church members and friends from other denominations, two ministers, Judge John V. Wright, Sunday School teachers, children of all ages, and members of the Masonic Order and Knights Templar, formed at the Masonic Hall and marched to the new church. Judge Wright delivered the dedication address.

This church was organized in 1820, and their first building, built soon after, was of frame construction on South Main Street. In 1836 a lot on Market and High Streets was purchased, and Nathan Vaught, a contractor, built what he called "a handsome structure."

A women's college was established in 1851 but was burned with many frame buildings in 1863 by the Union army. The church burned in April 1874 by accident. The next night the congregation gathered to make plans for a new building on the same site.

Architecturally, this church reflects Romanesque Revival styling and features fine stained glass windows. The large rose window honors the memory of President James K. Polk, who joined this church on his deathbed.

First United Methodist, Columbia

First United Methodist Church Cookeville

This Methodist church is believed to have been founded in 1855, and was listed in minutes of the Tennessee Conference in 1857. At that time, Ferdinand S. Petway was appointed presiding elder. Corna Freeman was appointed first pastor, and William Jared was appointed supply pastor.

The group held worship in the Putnam County courthouse until early 1857, when they began sharing a small, newly built house with other church groups.

In 1895 a lot on Spring Street near the present church site was bought, and a brick church was erected. This building was extensively remodeled in 1910 and used for worship until 1949, when the present church, an adaptation of Romanesque architecture, was completed. It was dedicated on November 23, 1952.

In 1913, the one hundredth anniversary session of the Tennessee Annual Conference met in this church. In 1955 this church, in cooperation with Tennessee Polytechnic Institute, again entertained the Annual Conference.

First United Methodist, Cookeville

Saint Peter's Episcopal Church Columbia

James Hervey Otey began holding religious services in Columbia in 1825, commuting from Franklin on horseback. The parochial reports in the Diocesan Journal for 1829 show that twelve communicants organized the second parish in Tennessee at Columbia. With the Reverend Daniel Stephens as the first rector, this small group worshipped in the Masonic Lodge Hall until their first church was completed in 1834.

Leonidas Polk graduated from the United States Military Academy at West Point and the Virginia Theological Seminary in Alexandria, Virginia, and then moved to Middle Tennessee, where he built a handsome home known as Ashwood near Columbia. He succeeded Daniel Stephens as rector of Saint Peter's Church and held the post until he was elected Bishop of the Southwest Missionary District comprising Arkansas, Oklahoma, and Texas. He later served as a general in the Confederate army.

The cornerstone was laid for a new church in 1860, but work was interrupted by the Civil War. The sixty communicants worshipped in the unfinished church until 1863, when Federal troops closed the building and used it as barracks and hospital for eighteen months.

When the troops evacuated the building they set fire to it, but John Baird, senior warden, discovered the blaze and extinguished it. As a result, Baird's family was harassed by Federal troops.

Saint Peter's church as it stands today was consecrated in 1871 by Bishop Charles Quintard. Memorial gifts, including the altar, chancel, pulpit, pews and stained glass windows, were received between 1868 and 1890.

Dr. Oertel, a priest and artist who lived in Columbia and Sewanee, painted "The Rock of Ages," which is believed to be the most copied painting in the world. He gave twenty paintings to the Columbia Institute, which closed in 1932; these paintings were then given to Saint Peter's Church. Appraisers have judged two of these to be valuable works of art.

Camille Herndon was confirmed on Palm Sunday, April 3, 1887. As organist at Saint Peter's she played her first service at age fourteen and continued in the post for sixty years. She raised the money for the purchase of the Kilgen organ installed in 1912 and for the heating system still in use, and gave her home to the Church Endowment Fund.

Saint Peter's Episcopal, Columbia

Cornersville United Methodist Church
Cornersville

One acre of ground was given by William Henderson to John Haynes, Holman Fowler, and Joseph Armar in February 1822 for the purpose of erecting a meeting house to be used by Methodist and Presbyterian churches. A Methodist meeting house was built near the center of the village of Cornersville sometime before 1846.

The cornerstone of the present building was laid on July 22, 1852 by Methodist ministers, assisted by members of the Masonic Lodge of Cornersville and of the Lodge from Pulaski. The lower floor of this church was then used by the church and the upper floor by the Masonic Lodge. This practice was common in all sections of Tennessee at the time. A deed of all claims to the church property was accepted from the Masonic Lodges in 1939.

At a meeting of the Tennessee Annual Conference in October, 1852, membership of the Cornersville church was stated as eighty-five: sixty White, twenty-five Black, eighteen on probation.

Cornersville United Methodist

Saint Matthew's Episcopal, Covington

Saint Matthew's Episcopal Church Covington

Saint Paul's Church at Randolph, Tennessee was organized in 1832 by Reverend Thomas Wright. It burned and was never rebuilt. Four families who had been Saint Paul members moved to Covington after the fire and became the nucleus of the congregation of Saint Matthew's Church.

The cornerstone for this church was laid in 1858. "Old Uncle" Shirley Fisher and other Fisher slaves sawed the yellow poplar and red gum lumber for the building by hand, using a crosscut saw. Mortised and pegged, the building rests on a stone foundation.

According to Ebenezer Paine, Bishop Charles Quintard was in England when extensive renovation was in progress at Canterbury Cathedral. He acquired three stained glass windows, believed to be nearly three hundred years old, which had been discarded. They were shipped by sailing vessel to New Orleans, up the Mississippi River to Randolph (near Memphis) then overland to Covington. The journey took six months.

Those windows were installed in Saint Matthew's and remain treasured possessions, chiefly because they were a gift from Bishop Quintard, who had preached in this church many times.

Mount Carmel Presbyterian, Covington

Mount Carmel Presbyterian Church
Covington

One of the finest nineteenth century churches in West Tennessee is Mount Carmel, which combines Gothic Revival and Greek Revival features. It was built in 1854 of frame construction, and is relatively unchaged from its original appearance. Sometime during the winter of 1834, twenty-four people met in the log home of Reverend James Holmes, a former missionary to the Chickasaw Indians in Mississippi. There a church was organized, money subscribed for a church building, and elders and deacons elected. During the time of building the church, the congregation worshipped in the stable where Holmes kept his horse. There is no description of this church, which burned after a few years.

The present church stands west of the original church on a low hill with landscaped grounds totaling about five acres. The roster of the new church contained the names of twenty-one White and three Black members. The Reverend Hugh Wilson, who had served with Holmes as a missionary in Mississippi, became the first pastor of the 1854 church.

In 1840, Holmes founded Mount Carmel Academy, which became one of the most important secondary schools in Tennessee. It offered separate schools and curricula for girls and boys who came from neighboring states. Students lived in the homes of church members. The school closed around 1900.

First Baptist, Dandridge

First Baptist Church
Dandridge

When this church was organized on March 25, 1786, it was called Lower French Broad Baptist Church. It is the oldest Baptist church in Jefferson County, and perhaps is the third oldest church in Tennessee in continuous existence. It was founded by Reverends Isaac Barton and Jonathan Mulkey in Cook's School House, three miles east of Dandridge, the only town in the United States bearing the maiden name of Martha Washington.

This congregation has preserved all of the church records since 1786. They are the oldest records of any kind in Jefferson County still intact.

Three other churches have been organized out of First Baptist at Dandridge—Dumplin (1797), Antioch (1813), and French Broad at Oak Grove (1887).

A former pastor, William Rogers, became the first President of Mossy Creek College, later Carson-Newman College, in Jefferson City. Member W. A Montgomery served as the first executive secretary of the Tennessee Baptist Convention.

A frame building erected in 1845 served this congregation until 1982, when the present Colonial structure was completed. Windows from the old church were moved into the new building.

Denmark Presbyterian

Denmark Presbyterian Church
Denmark

Denmark Church was organized by five men in 1821 on Cub Creek five miles from its present location. The church grew rapidly and moved in 1833 to Denmark, where a log school house was used by many denominations. Dissention developed between Presbyterians and the large Baptist group, and the Presbyterians erected their own building in six days and called it "Jonah's Gourd."

The present building was erected in 1854 with Reverend J.W. Gillaspis as the first pastor. He served twenty-seven years. His salary was $1,200 per year, an amount considered extravagant at the time.

In 1861, Reverend Gillaspis preached to a group called "Denmark Danes," who with their Captain John Ingram were presented a flag made by women of Denmark, and then marched to Jackson to join the Sixth Tennessee Regiment of the Confederate army. A bell, cast in North Carolina and said to contain silver given by the ladies of the church, tolled as the "Denmark Danes" marched away and again when they returned.

During the Civil War the churchyard became a Federal army bivouac. Tradition says that on one occasion, two of General Nathan Bedford Forrest's men were attending church with their sweethearts when a detachment of Federal soldiers entered and searched the building for the two men, who escaped by hiding under the hoop skirts of the young ladies.

The upper floor of Denmark Church was used by the Masonic Lodge for many years, and also served as prison for eighty-seven Federal soldiers who surrendered after the Battle of Britton's Lane.

John Murrell, an outlaw, lived south of Denmark and is said to have occupied the pulpit one Sunday morning in 1833 while his "mystic gang" stole the horses of the worshippers.

Dyersburg Methodist

United Methodist Church
Dyersburg

The first church built in Dyer County was a frame building in the village of Ro-Ellen in 1830. It served Baptists, Cumberland Presbyterians, and Methodists.

In 1842, the Methodist Church was organized in Dyersburg with Robert McKendree Tarrant as minister. His ancestors had immigrated from England to New Jersey and claimed a large grant of land in 1681.

A small frame building was built by the group in 1844, and sometime before 1890 a brick church was constructed at the corner of Mill and Church Streets. The present building was completed in 1923 on McGaughey Street.

Dyersburg was made a station of the Conference in 1855, with Jack Mahon as "preacher in charge."

Members and friends arrived at the church early and visited on the grounds, awaiting the sound of a conch shell blown to announce worship. On entering the church, men sat on the right side and women on the left. It was considered scandalous for an unmarried couple to ride alone in a buggy to church, but two or more unmarried couples could ride to church in a surrey.

First Baptist, Dyersburg

First Baptist Church
Dyersburg

James H. Borum moved with his family from Prince Edward County, Virginia, to Wilson County, Tennessee, when he was twelve years old. The family later moved to Tipton County, where he preached his first sermon at age twenty at Liberty School and Meeting House. On July 2, 1867, he founded the Baptist Church of Dyersburg with twenty-eight charter members. He died in 1888 at age 72 and is buried in the Old City Cemetery.

For three years the group worshipped in Hess Lodge Building on Mill Avenue. In 1870 arrangements were made to meet in the Presbyterian church. They built a church and dedicated it in 1879 with James H. Borum as pastor.

Around 1900, the church divided and formed two congregations, First Baptist and Dyersburg Baptist. These two groups were reunited in 1903 and took the name Union Missionary Baptist Church. They worshipped in the brick building erected by the Dyersburg Baptists and dedicated sometime after 1900.

In 1919, the Walker property on the corner of Church and Masonic Streets was purchased by the church; the present Greek Revival church was built there and dedicated in 1929. The name was changed to First Baptist Church of Dyersburg in 1928.

Sinking Creek Baptist, Elizabethton

Sinking Creek Baptist Church
Elizabethton

Sinking Creek Baptist Church is the oldest church building still standing in Tennessee. The congregation was organized in 1772 by Matthew Talbot, and the building was erected the next year of logs cut on the site.

An Indian uprising in the area forced the group to abandon the church until 1777, when Talbot, John Mulkey, and Joshua Kelley returned and resumed worship services. In the interval, a member of Sinking Creek Church named McDowell was scalped by the Indians.

In 1869, this church joined the Watauga Association, and in 1884 the Association met here for the first time.

The church was restored and enlarged in 1924, and new Sunday School rooms were added in 1940. A new church was built near the old one in 1962. The log building was sold to the Sinking Creek Baptist Church Historical Society, which has restored it to the original design and appearance. It is now enshrined as a special property of the Watauga Association of the Baptist Church.

First Presbyterian, Fayetteville

First Presbyterian Church
Fayetteville

Three years after Lincoln County was organized, Reverend John Gillespie founded First Presbyterian Church here. The year was 1812 and the new congregation worshipped in the courthouse until 1832, when the first church was completed. It was destroyed by a storm in 1851.

The present church was completed in 1854; an original two-columned portico and tall steeple were removed in 1866 and were never replaced.

In 1917, Albert P. Woodard, Atlanta architect, designed extensive alterations in keeping with the classic style of the building.

Fayetteville Church of Christ
Fayetteville

Dr. John McKinney and family and John Goodrich and wife, assisted by Talbot Fanning and C. R. Darnell, founded this church in 1835. The congregation was forty-nine years old before it had a house of worship of its own.

That first brick building was erected in 1889 and destroyed by a cyclone in 1890. Its second church was destroyed by a tornado in 1952. The present building of Greco-Romanesque architecture was erected in 1952.

Fayetteville Church of Christ

First Baptist Church
Franklin

"We know little of the early history of the Franklin Baptist Church except the great trials, turmoil and division which overtook it in those early days. On this point, we doubt if any church in the United States since the establishment of religious liberty has had to pass through such great trials," wrote Dr. E. P. Alldredge in the 1922 *Southern Baptist Handbook*.

Three lots were bought on April 4, 1800, to establish a Baptist Church and a school in Franklin. The traditional date for the church founding, however, has always been the first Sunday of February in 1830.

Although torn apart over the question of missions in 1838, the membership stood at 440 in 1851 under the leadership of Reverend J. E. Graves.

During that same year, Alexander Campbell made a visit to Franklin and was given the use of the Baptist church for preaching. A short time later, when he asked for a vote to see who wanted to follow him, all but four members left the Baptist Church. Two months later, two of the remaining four moved away. The last two, Deacon John C. Wells and his daughter, met at the deserted church regularly to sing and pray. Gradually the membership grew, only to lose all its men in the Civil War.

The Federal army seized this church for use as a hospital, and when it was returned to the congregation at the end of the war the building was in bad condition. It burned in 1890 or 1891, leaving only blackened walls.

Through the efforts of the Reverend L. B. Jarmon and Mrs. Betty Thomas, both of whom gave their entire time and energy to the task, the church was rebuilt. The stained glass windows are some of the most beautiful in Middle Tennessee.

First Baptist, Franklin

Saint Paul's Episcopal Church Franklin

"Mother of the Episcopal Diocese of Tennessee," this church was formally organized on August 25, 1827 by James Hervey Otey. This red brick building with arched windows and a square tower has a simple dignity reminiscent of old English churches.

Otey was born in Virginia and graduated with honors from the University of North Carolina at age 20. He was sent to Middle Tennessee in 1825 to further the growth of the Episcopal church, and established Harpeth Academy in Franklin. The founder of Episcopalianism in Tennessee, he was elected bishop in 1834.

The handsome interior was badly defaced and abused during the Civil War, when it was used as a barracks and a hospital by the Union army and, later, the Confederate army. When hostilities had ceased, the building was repaired, and, in some respects, its appearance was drastically changed. The front entrance was moved to the opposite end from its former location, and the altar was moved to the former front of the building. New pews, a new pipe organ, a new altar, and exquisite Tiffany windows have been added. The church was reconsecrated by Bishop Charles Quintard in 1871.

The iron fence encircling the grounds was bought from the First Presbyterian Church when that church was razed in 1887.

Saint Paul's Episcopal, Franklin

Fourth Avenue Church of Christ
Franklin

In 1830, when the temperature was near zero, Alexander Campbell preached in the Baptist Church, the Presbyterian Church, and the Masonic Hall where Episcopalians were worshipping. In 1833, Joel Anderson and Andrew Craig preached in Franklin, and later that year, Absalom Adams and Tolbert Fanning organized the Chruch of Christ in Franklin with seventeen members.

In 1836, a building lot was purchased; the deed was registered in 1838. The first house of worship was begun in 1851, and the first service was held there September 5, 1852. Two sermons lasting two hours were delivered to four hundred listeners.

The building was made of brick and featured arched windows, a bell tower, and two front doors. It was damaged during the Civil War by Union troops, who used it for barracks and a hospital. It was not restored until 1885.

In 1914, the building was renovated and a larger one created. It was an unusual style with a long octagonal tower and arches on the front. It was damaged by a tornado in 1926 and razed in 1927. The third church, on the same site, was built in a vernacular Greek Revival style and served the congregation until 1978, when the present building of modified Greek Revival style was completed and the old one was demolished. The stained glass windows originally installed in the 1928 one are now in the present church.

The bell which hangs in a small tower in the present church hung in the original church built in 1852, and in the second building of 1914. While the third building was under construction in 1927, the bell was sold and the proceeds placed in the general fund. In 1930, members expressed a desire to locate the bell and place it in the church again. Dr. Horace German led a search for it and a Mr. Fox, who had purchased it, gave it to the church.

During the influenza epidemic of 1918 when indoor meetings were banned, the members of this church met regularly for worship on the front steps.

This church has been known as Franklin Church of Christ, Downtown Church of Christ, Christian Church, and, since 1950, Fourth Avenue Church of Christ.

Fourth Avenue Church of Christ, Franklin

First Baptist Church
Gallatin

With many citizens holding membership in Baptist churches in other towns, the Reverend J. R. Graves organized a Baptist church in Gallatin in March 1859, with twelve members. The first church building was dedicated on July 1, 1860.

Soon after the church began functioning the Civil War interrupted the worship here and the new building became a miliary hospital. When the war was over, the church was restored; the congregation worshipped here until 1887, when the building was destroyed by fire. There was no insurance coverage on the church.

While a new house of worship was being built the Gallatin Baptist congregation worshipped in a building known locally as the "Open House." The new church, a landmark in Gallatin, served this congregation until 1949, when the present church of Greek Revival architecture was completed. Featuring columns on a recessed portico, this church has a simple cross atop the front end but no steeple.

Southside Baptist Church and Indian Hills Church were former missions of Gallatin First Baptist Church.

First Baptist, Gallatin

First United Methodist, Gallatin

First United Methodist Church Gallatin

The first church in Gallatin was a union church on Bledsoe Street, built in 1804; the churchyard there became the Gallatin Cemetery. The membership numbered 125.

In 1829, the Methodists decided to build their own church. Soon members of other denominations made the same decision, and the Union Church on Bledsoe Street was given to the Black members.

During the Civil War the Methodist church was used as a hospital. In 1866, a great revival was experienced, and in eight years the membership had grown to such proportions that the present church was built in 1874.

The first organist in this church was Louise King, age ten, playing on a small cottage organ. Some men disliked the organ music and would enter the church with stern expressions on their faces and sing extremely loudly to drown the sound of the organ. A reed pump organ was placed in the gallery, and a pipe organ was installed later. Louise King became Mrs. Peacock of Chattanooga, and was present for the centennial celebration of the church in 1929.

First Presbyterian Church Gallatin

This church grew out of a series of sacramental meetings led by Reverend John W. Hall in the summer of 1828 at Shiloh and at the Gallatin non-denominational Union churches. It was organized on October 25, 1828 with 77 charter members. Hall was assisted in the organization by Dr. Gideon Blackburn, then President of Centre College, Danville, Kentucky, and Reverend Jacob B. Crisp of the Methodist Church.

Hall became the first pastor in April 1830. He was a commissioner from the Shiloh Presbytery to meetings of the General Assembly in the First Presbyterian Church in Philadelphia in 1828 and 1832.

The Greek Revival church dates from 1836. The two round Doric columns are brick covered with stucco, as are the two square pilasters on the recessed porch, which was more deeply recessed originally and featured an arched doorway. Part of the porch was enclosed in 1958 to form a narthex.

The sanctuary is unchanged since the early twentieth century. The Gothic wood pews face a semi-circular rostrum and pipe organ installed in 1915. The organ, featuring an Egyptian Revival motif, was removed from Downtown Presbyterian Church in Nashville and installed here.

Pleasant Mount Cumberland Presbyterian Church
Glendale

Located on a shady knoll above Fountain Creek east of Glendale, this church was built by a Mr. Fisher of Franklin in 1899 to replace an earlier frame building. There is an iron-fenced cemetery in the churchyard.

The interior design of this Gothic Revival church features natural oak floors, pews, and balustrades original to the building. Lancet-shaped window sashes flanking the entrance to the church are patterned after old tracery designs used in thirteenth century English Gothic churches.

The first building here was built in 1868 and served as both church and school for children of the area. Known as Pleasant Mount Academy, this school continued for thirty years.

First Presbyterian, Gallatin

Connell Memorial United Methodist Church
Goodlettsville

Mansker's fort on Mansker Creek, one mile north of Goodlettsville, was on the preaching circuit of Benjamin Ogden in 1797. In 1800, a log meeting house was built on six acres of land given by Isaac Walton, a prominent citizen. It was known as Walton's Camp Ground and the church there was in use until 1805, when a larger one was built.

In 1830, the old church was torn down and replaced by a frame building on two acres of land two miles away in Goodlettsville. This move occurred while John Sherrill, E. P. Connell, and his wife Nancy, who was the daughter of Isaac Walton, were pastoring the church.

The present Gothic Revival church was erected in 1905 during the ministry of Reverend W. L. Jackson, and included the sanctuary and three classrooms. A small pedal pump organ provided music until 1908, when the Carnegie Foundation provided a grant for one half the price of a pipe organ. The remaining funds were raised by the Women's Society, who held bazaars, ice cream suppers, and other individual projects.

Pleasant Mount Cumberland Presbyterian

Connell Memorial United Methodist, Goodlettsville

Saint James Episcopal, Greeneville

Saint James Episcopal
Greeneville

This white Gothic style frame church was designed by George M. Spencer. Typical of Episcopal architecture in Tennessee of the period, it was completed in 1850 and dedicated by Bishop James Hervey Otey. This small congregation had been formed in 1842.

The sanctuary, featuring walnut woodwork and pews, retains its architectural integrity and appearance. The organ is believed to be the oldest church organ still in use in Tennessee. A gallery for slaves also remains.

During the Civil War, General John Hunt Morgan hid in this church before his death in 1864.

Asbury United Methodist Church
Greeneville

The name Asbury was chosen for this church because in 1790 Bishop Asbury was a guest in the Maloney Hotel, which stood on the site of the present church.

Methodist activity began in Greeneville in 1820. Land was bought in March 1821 on Irish Street, on which Mount Moriah Methodist Episcopal Church was built. In 1849 it was sold and another lot bought for the site of the Methodist Episcopal Church, South.

In 1866, reorganization resulting from a split in the membership left six members in the original congregation. The others formed the Methodist Episcopal Church, later known as "Northern Methodist." They moved the church furniture into the Greene County courthouse, where they worshipped for many years, although they held possession of the old church.

In 1874, the Methodist Episcopal Church, South, brought a lawsuit in Chancery Court and were granted possession of the building. Later the Tennessee Supreme Court upheld that decision.

In 1873, the Methodist Episcopal Church was organized; the following year the Maloney Hotel was purchased. A portion of the hotel served as a parsonage for a time, and a large frame church with a tall steeple was built on part of the property in 1875. That church was in use until 1910, when along with the parsonage it was moved to another part of the lot to make room for a new church. That old frame building was later sold and became a garage and, later, a tobacco barn.

The cornerstone for the present sanctuary was laid on October 2, 1911. On April 12, 1912, the stately brick church was opened for worship, dedicated, and presented to the Holston Conference. The name Asbury Memorial Methodist Church was adopted at that time.

Stained glass windows in this church are outstanding. The water-powered Estey pipe organ was installed in 1911 and has since been electrified. It was rebuilt in 1955 and is still in use.

Asbury Methodist, Greeneville

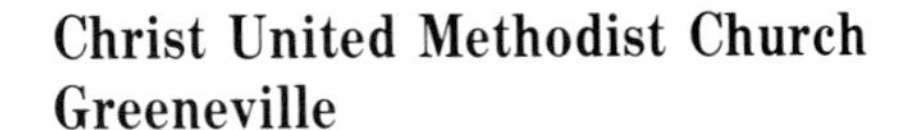

Christ United Methodist Church
Greeneville

Organized March 10, 1821, as Mount Moriah, this group soon purchased land in Greeneville as a site for a Methodist church. In 1849 the land on which the present church stands was acquired and a frame building was erected. It was burned about 1850 by an angry slave.

A brick building replacing the burned frame one also burned about 1880. The present Gothic church was built after 1890. Renovations and expansions were made in 1922 and again in 1957. In 1968, the name was changed to Christ United Methodist Church.

Unusual stained glass windows are among the treasures in this church.

Christ United Methodist, Greeneville

New Bethel Cumberland Presbyterian Church
Greeneville

Led by Thomas Davis, Philip Eblezier, and William E. Davis, thirty-eight Greene County citizens petitioned the Knoxville Presbytery of the Cumberland Presbyterian Church for organization of a church to be known as New Bethel congregation.

James Carter, whose ambition was to enter the ministry, died before he could realize that ambition, and bequeathed funds for a church to be built on a four-acre tract of land donated by John Harmon in 1841. The new church was built in 1842-43 in the vernacular Gothic Revival style, which was used frequently in rural churches in East and Middle Tennessee before the Civil War. Only a few churches of this type remain in Tennessee, and New Bethel is an excellent example.

Oil lamps have been replaced by electricity and some other modernizations have been added, but the church's overall appearance is otherwise much the same as it was more than a century ago.

New Bethel Cumberland Presbyterian, Greeneville

First Presbyterian Church
Hendersonville

A commission was formed from the Nashville Presbytery to establish a congregation in Hendersonville. Reverend Henry Buckner Broude, Reverend James W. Hoyt, Dr. George Thompson and John M. Lawrence organized the church and chose a building site on Main Street.

The first pastor here in this original church building was Reverend Alexander Cowan of Shelbyville, who came here thirty years old and unmarried. Later Tabitha Wherry, daughter of Elder and Mrs. John J. Wherry, became his wife.

Nestled in a quiet grove of trees, this vernacular Gothic building was erected in 1869. It is partially surrounded by an old cemetery in which nine Civil War veterans, including General Daniel Smith Donelson, are buried. Burial lots here were sold to help defray the expense of building the church.

First Presbyterian Church
Greenfield

"The Church of Ebenezer," meaning "stone of help," was organized in Greenfield in 1837 and is believed to have been the first church founded there. The first elder was Jessie Foust, Sr.

One acre of land was given by Joe H. Ward for a church site, and soon a building of handmade boards with a cypress timber roof was completed. Materials and labor were donated by members, in such measure that only three hundred dollars was spent on the building.

In 1870 this congregation joined the Cumberland Presbyterian Church. In 1897 the frame building was demolished and a two story brick church was erected.

Soon after 1900, the congregation divided and two were formed, one Cumberland Presbyterian, the other Presbyterian, U.S.A. The 1897 church was destroyed by fire and furnishings and records were lost. The present church of Greek Revival architecture, featuring a series of memorial windows, was erected in 1920.

Mr. W.O. Elam, who had served this church as an elder for 77 years, died in 1957.

First Presbyterian, Greenfield

First Presbyterian, Hendersonville

Old Hermitage Presbyterian Church
Hermitage

Hermitage Presbyterian Church began in a small log building used for both school and worship in 1816. This structure burned in 1818. Returning to the Hermitage in 1823, President and Mrs. Jackson felt the need for a church in the area, and, along with five friends, contributed $680 of the necessary $800. The remainder was donated by local settlers, and the building was constructed soon after. It measured thirty by fifty feet, with brick walls eighteen inches thick.

The church was plain, featuring a brick floor, hard benches arranged in a semi-circle around a pulpit, and a fireplace in each end. It was dedicated in 1824 by Reverend William Hume with nine signing members, including Mrs. Rachel Jackson. The name "Ephesus" was chosen for this first church.

President Jackson was perhaps motivated in his interest in this religious venture by Mrs. Jackson's long time desire for a house of worship, but records do not substantiate the story that he built the church for her. Rachel was a devout Presbyterian whose Virginia ancestors were prominent in that faith. President Jackson was a member of this church.

Occupied and badly damaged by Union troops during the Civil War, it was repaired under the direction of Mrs. Bettie M. Donelson in 1889. Money for this project was raised in part by a series of "Old Folks" concerts.

The church was gutted by fire in 1965, although the walls, brick floor, and chimneys were not seriously damaged. The congregation built a new building at the corner of Old Hickory Boulevard and Lebanon Road, and the Ladies Hermitage Association took over the restoration of "Rachel's Chapel."

Research was done by Mrs. Douglas Henry of Nashville and architect Hardie Bass for authenticity. The church was restored to its 1837-45 condition in 1969, and plans for a future museum have been made. The late Judge William E. Miller conducted a naturalization ceremony here, and weddings are held here on occasion.

Long Rock United Methodist, Huntingdon

Old Hermitage Presbyterian, Hermitage

Andrews Chapel Methodist Church
Huntersville

This rural church, named in honor of Bishop Andrews, was established in 1820. Major James Meriweather served on the building committee and supervized the cutting and hewing of logs from a neaby forest with a crude rip saw. The labor was performed by slaves.

Andrews Chapel stands on a broad expanse of land surrounded by beautiful old trees. A large and well-maintained cemetery is nearby. The building is the original and is in a fine state of preservation.

Andrews Chapel Methodist, Huntersville

Long Rock United Methodist Church
Huntingdon

Early records show that a small wooden church known as Oak Grove stood on the present-day Long Rock School grounds as early as 1874. A deed, dated 1886, states that members of Oak Grove Church and other interested citizens burned brick in a kiln nearby and built the brick church which stands now. The later name "Long Rock" derives from a nearby geological formation.

The building of this church was truly a community project. Each family donated one cord of wood to be burned in the kiln where the bricks were fired; enough bricks were made for the church and a school house built at a later date. Women and children, including girls, cultivated cotton patches of one quarter acre each and donated all the money from their crop to the building fund. In this way, they raised one hundred forty dollars.

The original pews and pulpit are still in use. A large bell used to call the people to church, to announce deaths in the community, and to call for men to assemble at the nearby cemeteries to dig graves is on the grounds today.

In earlier times the church was served by circuit riding preachers, one of whom, Reverend J.H. Witt, rode a mule to the churches on his circuit. He frequently stopped along the way and preached in homes. The first regular pastor of Long Rock was Reverend H.B. Johnson.

First Baptist, Huntingdon

First United Methodist, Huntingdon

First Baptist Church
Huntingdon

With twenty-three charter members, Reverend G. L. Ellis organized the Huntingdon Baptist Church on December 31, 1888, in the Cumberland Presbyterian Church. The original red brick sanctuary of Gothic design was erected the next year and Reverend Mr. Ellis became the first pastor. The site for the church was donated by Judge Joe R. Hawkins, saying that although he was not a churchman, he would not live in a town which had no churches.

In 1898, G.W. Elleston and W.T. Rose were ordained to preach in Huntingdon Baptist, and Reverend Bernard Scates became the first full-time pastor. The first educational building was erected during his pastorate.

In 1955, the original building was razed and the present church, standing on the original site, was built in an adaptation of Gothic Revival design. In 1963, Mr. Sam Kennon donated a large tract of land at the rear of the building for additional educational space.

First United Methodist Church
Huntingdon

As early as 1840, a Methodist society was meeting in Huntingdon. It was July 1877 when the Huntingdon Methodist Church South was organized in a small frame building on Main Street at Third Avenue. It is believed to have been the first denomination to organize here after the Civil War.

In 1879, the Methodist congregation exchanged their property on Main Street for one nearer the business district on Main Street between Second and Third; the Christian congregation had begun to build a house of worship here but had abandoned the project. In 1910 this Victorian Gothic red brick church was rebuilt, and extensive renovations were made in 1945-48.

In 1967, plans began for construction of a new church at another site. Hart, Freeland, and Roberts, a Nashville architectural company, was engaged to design and supervise construction, and contractor Sam Barger of Huntingdon built the stone church of vernacular adaptation of Romanesque architecture. Old stained glass windows from the church on Main Street were placed in the new one.

On September 20, 1970, a deconsecration service was held in the old church by trustees. All sacramental elements were removed and, followed by the congregation, were carried to the new sanctuary on Highway 22, where a dedication service was held.

Governor Gordon Browning was a member of this church for fifty years and was a member of the Board of Stewards.

Saint Luke's Episcopal
Jackson

Organized in 1832, this congregation did not complete their church until 1845. It was consecrated in 1853 by Bishop James Otey.

In 1870, after he was released from prison, Jefferson Davis delivered an address here. The church proved inadequate to accommodate all who came to hear him, and the group moved outside, where a still larger crowd had gathered in a grove in front of the home of General Samuel J. Hayes.

An exquisite cross on the altar and an alms basin still in use were given to this church by Bishop Charles Quintard, who had received them from the Duchess of Tesk while traveling in England. These priceless objects are said to have been copied from those in Westminster Abbey.

A treasured communion service, a carved quartered oak reredos enclosing a painting of the Resurrection, and triple mosaic windows in the rear of the building are a few of the relics and treasures of this handsome church.

First Baptist, Jackson

First Methodist, Jackson

Saint Luke's Episcopal, Jackson

irst Baptist Church
ackson

ı a short history of this church by Deacon Henry
lay Irby, the first building of this congregation is
escribed as "a market house which stood at the
orthwest corner of Market Street (now Highland
venue) and College Street, which was fitted out
nd served its purpose."

The church was organized with twelve members
n January 29, 1837, with founding elders John
'inlay, who became the first pastor, and Peter S.
ayle, the third pastor. In 1847, a second building
eplaced the "market house." A third church was
ompleted in 1910.

Pastor W.C. Boone became executive secretary of
he Kentucky Baptist Convention, and Dr. Fred
endall became executive secretary of the
'ennessee Baptist Convention. During the pastorate
f Dr. Wayne Dehoney in 1957-67, the television
ninistry was begun. Morning worship services have
een televised without interruption since then.

A new church of Neoclassical architecture was
edicated on August 24, 1980. It stands near the site
f the original church and features a wealth of
nusual stained glass. The membership here is
pproaching 3,500.

'irst Methodist Church
ackson

oon after the Chickasaw Purchase in October 1818,
he Tennessee Annual Conference appointed two
Iethodist missionaries, Reverends Hezekiah Holland
nd Lewis Garrett, to the region. In 1821, they
eported 146 White and thirteen Black Methodists in
ne district.

In 1822 a presiding elder's district was established.
ne outstanding elder in those early times was Dr.
.W.D. Harris, brother of Governor Isham Harris
nd Supreme Court Justice William R. Harris.

In 1826, three years after Jackson became an
ıcorporated town, a Methodist church was organized
nder the leadership of Reverend Thomas Neely
vith eight members. The organizational meeting took
lace in the new log courthouse at the southeast
orner of Court Square. In 1831, the first house of
'orship was built on the corner of Chester and
'hurch Streets, across the street from the site of the
resent church.

In 1851, the small church was sold to the "Jackson
ons of Temperance" and a lot across the street was
urchased. There a brick church was built, with
rown Brothers and Newell as contractors.

In 1840, the Memphis Conference was established,
nd the first session of that body met in Jackson.
ince that time the Memphis conference has met in
ackson close to twenty times.

First Methodist Church was used as a stable by the Union army during the Civil War, while worship was carried on in the Masonic Lodge hall. The government reimbursed First Methodist Church for Civil War damages in 1885.

In 1912, First Methodist Church, regarded as one of the most beautiful in the South, was destroyed by fire. The present church of Greco-Romanesque architecture was completed and formally opened on September 6, 1914, with Bishop William D. Murrah conducting the service.

A marble baptismal font imported from Italy, standing outside the chancel rail, is a memorial to Reverend William G. Hefley, a former presiding elder of this district. At the altar, six handmade communion kneelers have been placed. Made in basket weave stitch, the kneelers and seats of pulpit chairs and a kneeler for use at weddings are all memorials and depict symbolic decorations adapted from the stained glass windows in the sanctuary.

First Presbyterian Church
Jackson

Organized in 1823 by a supply pastor named Hall, First Presbyterian Church had no full time pastor and no regular meeting place for almost ten years. The first church was erected in 1832 on the corner of Main and Church Streets. A brick building painted gray, it was the first church in Jackson.

The building lot was donated by the first pastor, Dr. Alexander Augustus Campbell, who was born in Amherst, Virginia, in December 1789. He studied medicine in Philadelphia, and practiced as a physician in North Carolina, Virginia and Alabama. He had been an infidel for many years and became a Christian during an attack of yellow fever. Pastor of First Presbyterian Church in Jackson from 1833 until 1846, he also edited a paper called the *Jackson Protestant*.

During the Civil War, worship services were discontinued while the Union army occupied the church. The building was not repaired until 1881. It was demolished in 1912 and a church of Greek Revival style was erected on the same site. The exterior was made of Indiana limestone, and inside wainscoting and floors were of Tennessee marble. Windows of leaded glass featured Easter lilies at the bottom. This building was sold to Second National Bank in 1956, and the bank is now located there.

On May 27, 1957, a new sanctuary of Colonial architecture was dedicated on North Highland Avenue on eight and a half wooded acres of land given by Mrs. Clarence Pigford in memory of her husband. Included in the gift was the Pigford home, "Chevy Chase," now named Memorial Hall.

The Memorial Carillon Tower was the first building on the new site, and was dedicated on September 12, 1954. The tower contains forty-seven bells forged in France by Les Fils de G. Paccard. The bells were installed in Jackson under the supervision of Arthur Bigelow of Princeton University. The carillon was erected by members of First Presbyterian Church and other citizens of Jackson and Madison County in memory of those who served in World Wars I and II.

The tower, sanctuary, and other buildings of First Presbyterian church were designed by Harold E. Wagoner, architect.

First Presbyterian, Jackson

McKendree Methodist, Jasper

McKendree Methodist Episcopal Church, South Jasper

As early as 1809, Reverend Milton Ladd, a Methodist Circuit Rider, was preaching in the Jasper area. Many Circuit Riders were to follow him before Methodists in this small town purchased land for their church in 1870. They named it McKendree Methodist Church in honor of the first American-born Methodist Bishop.

Pryor Institute, named for General Jackson Pryor, one of its principal benefactors, was built in 1887 and opened in 1889. Dr. E. B. Craighead served as President of the school, which was in operation for twenty-one years under the auspices of the Holston Conference. In 1910 the building was sold to the County Board of Education and functioned for many years as Marion County High School.

The 1887 church was renovated in 1910-11 and was used for over ninety years; for many years it was the oldest building in use in the Holston conference of the United Methodist Church. Today the congregation meets in a new structure of contemporary architecture.

Central Baptist, Johnson City

entral Baptist Church
ohnson City

nown as First Baptist Church when it was founded n July 3, 1869, this congregation worshipped in irst Presbyterian Church until May 1881, and later the upper story of Science Hill Male and Female nstitute for a time. In April 1883 they moved to a uilding on East Main Street. Fire destroyed verything around this church in May 1905, but the uilding was spared.

In 1907, one hundred members organized Roan treet Baptist church and began meeting in Lusk chool at North Roan and Watauga Avenue. This hurch and First Baptist merged in 1910 and took he name Central Baptist Church. They moved into a ew church building on Thanksgiving Day, 1913.

In late December 1930, fire destroyed the interior f the church; worship was then held in the Junior ligh School nearby. The building was restored and s in use today.

The morning after the fire, Dr. William Rigell, 'astor, was standing on the sidewalk in front of the till smoldering building when a twelve year old boy topped beside him and said, "That fire sure burned he hell out of this church." Dr. Rigell's reply was "I ure hope so, son."

)owntown Christian Church
'ohnson City

'welve persons met in the home of William H. 'oung on November 12, 1871, and organized the hristian Church in Johnson City.

On June 29, 1872, Mr. Young deeded one acre of is farm to the congregation for a church site. The ocation was deemed undesirable for the purpose and vas sold; the money was applied on the first building f the Christian church in downtown Johnson City. 'his building was dedicated in 1879 and was lestroyed by fire in May 1905.

The Christian congregation worshipped in Jobe's)pera House for more than a year. The Opera House vas then condemned, and the church moved into a mall chapel on the corner of Main and Roan Streets. 'he present white brick church was dedicated June 0, 1906.

In 1972, First Christian Church moved to a new uilding on Sherwood Drive, near the Appalachian 'hristian Village. A part of the congregation chose o remain in the old church, and after buying the uilding changed the name to Downtown Christian 'hurch.

Downtown Christian, Johnson City

First Presbyterian Church
Jonesboro

Hebron Presbyterian Church was founded in 1790 by Samuel Doak and Hezekiah Balch. The congregation worshipped in a small log building, in which school was held during the summer months.

In 1816, Hebron Church moved into Jonesboro and purchased a building lot between Second Avenue and Washington Drive on the north side of Main Street. On this site a two-story building was erected. The upper floor was used for worship services, and the lower one was used by Martin Academy.

More land was procured and a larger building begun in 1831. The Holston Conference met there in 1831, although the building was not completed until 1836. In 1840, the name of the church was changed to Jonesboro Presbyterian.

The present Greek Revival church was constructed in 1850. Plans for the building drawn by Mr. Clise, a Kingsport architect, called for wide outside front steps, but feminine modesty demanded a change. Hoop skirts revealed the female ankle as ladies climbed the wide stairs up to the sanctuary. The outside steps became inside steps by enclosing the terrace from which the steps rose.

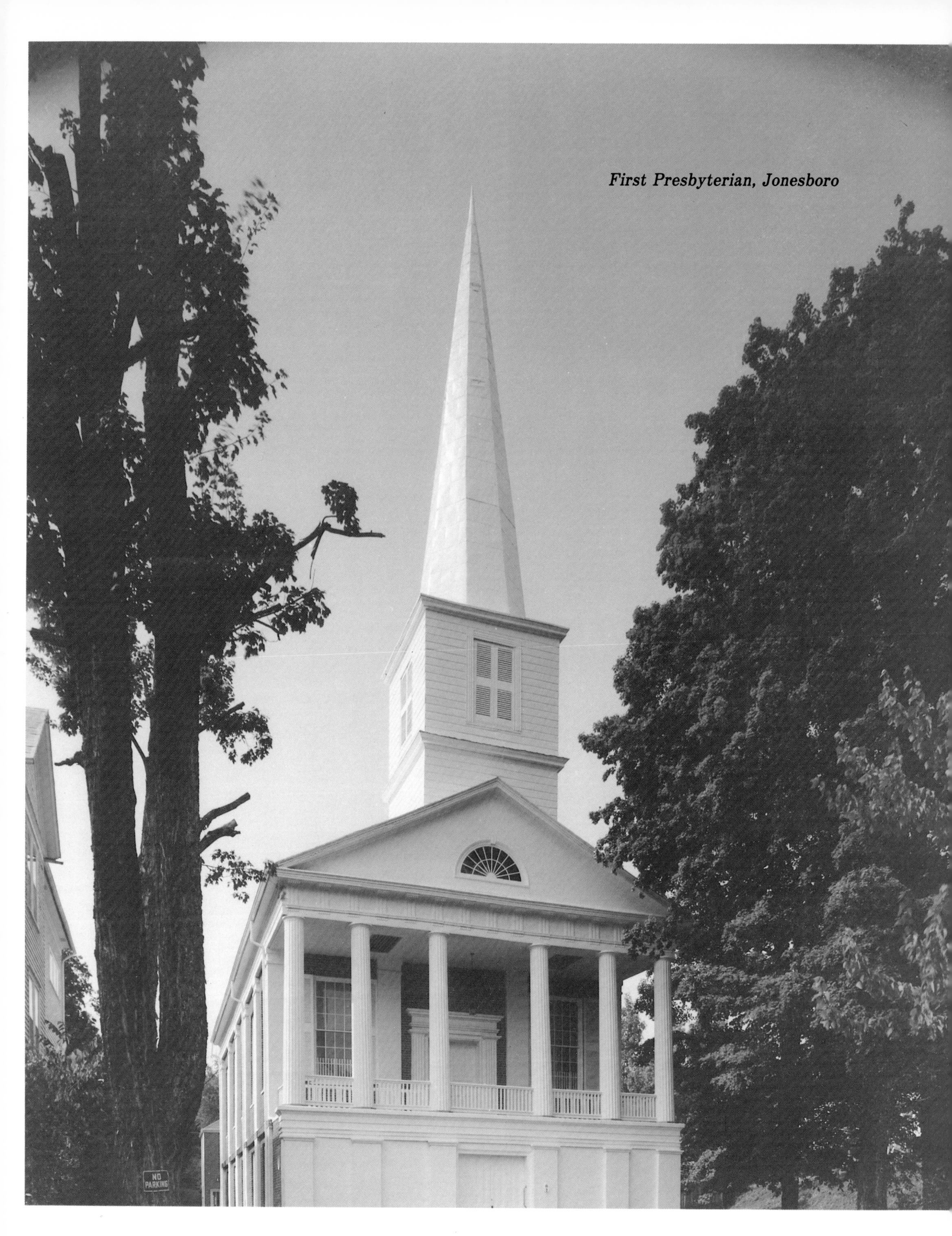

First Presbyterian, Jonesboro

The walnut pews originally were owned, and could be used by no one but the owner. Pew doors showing hinge marks and numbers remain in the present sanctuary. The bricks and window shutters were handmade, and they along with the wide floor boards and unusual hardware are original.

The altar is a replica of one in a northern Presbyterian church. The pulpit is reached by steps on each side, and the original slave gallery has been connected to a choir loft. The communion service and offering plates date from 1860.

First Baptist Church
Jonesboro

Matthew Talbot was preaching to groups at Sycamore Shoals on the Watauga River while Jonathan Mulkey worked among scattered groups in other locales in Washington County as early as 1775. In 1779, Tidence Lane organized Buffalo Ridge Baptist Church, and also served as its pastor. Nearly half a century later in 1842, a Baptist church was founded in Jonesboro, the oldest town in Tennessee.

William Cate, first pastor of the thirty-five member Baptist church, preached to his congregation in a small shed located on Spring Street while the brick Greek Revival church, completed in 1852, was under construction.

In 1853, through the efforts of Reverend William Cate, a school for girls opened under the direction of Mr. and Mrs. R. H. Keeling. Classes were held in the church until a large brick school building was erected on East Main Street near the church. The school prospered, but was closed shortly after the outbreak of the Civil War.

An epidemic of Asiatic cholera spread through the area in 1873. Many fled to other parts of the state, and of those who remained in the town it was estimated that one third died of the disease. Reverend G. C. Thrasher remained throughout the epidemic, ministering to the sick and bereaved. He is believed to have been the last victim to die of the disease in Jonesboro.

First Baptist, Jonesboro

Salem Presbyterian Church
Jonesboro

In 1780, Charles Cummings and Reverend Samuel Doak founded four churches in what is now East Tennessee—Salem Presbyterian Church near Jonesboro, Mount Bethel near Greeneville, Carter's Valley near Church Hill, and New Providence in Hawkins County. Carter's Valley Church no longer exists.

Salem Church is therefore one of the three oldest Presbyterian congregations in the state in continuous existence. Samuel Doak, pastor of this church and a true believer in the Presbyterian zeal for education, soon constructed a small log school house, known locally as "Doak's log cabin school." It became Martin College in 1783.

Reverend Doak rode his horse to New England and solicited aid for his new college. Among other gifts, Doak's friends contributed many books for the Martin College Library. He was said to have walked the five hundred miles to Jonesboro while his horse carried the books.

John Sevier, only governor of the "State of Franklin," second governor of Tennessee, and first representative to the United States Congress from west of the Allegheny Mountains, was among the first trustees of Martin College.

The college was the first institution of higher learning west of the Allegheny Mountains — thirteen years older than the State of Tennessee — and was chartered by three governments, North Carolina, the "State of Franklin," and United States South of the Ohio River. It was the chief school west of the Alleghenies for the study of law, medicine, and the ministry. Its name was later changed to Washington College, in honor of George Washington.

In 1818, Samuel Doak founded Tusculum College near Greeneville. His son, John W. Doak, served as its President. John Doak and James Witherspoon were the first graduates of Washington College in 1796, and thus became the first persons in Tennessee to earn the Bachelor of Arts degrees. The college near Jonesboro was merged with Tusculum College at Greeneville, and Washington College became a high school, which is still functioning.

Salem Church, on the Washington College campus, is worshipping in its third building. It was begun in 1895, and much of the construction work was done by students and faculty, who molded and fired the brick. Two round brick columns made by them remain. The yellow pine beams across the sanctuary are hand-hewn.

The rose window in the church is one of only three of its kind in the United States. The names of the Doak men can be found in the memorial stained glass windows.

Salem Presbyterian, Jonesboro

Jonesboro United Methodist Church
Jonesboro

Jonesboro Methodist was founded in 1822 as a result of a series of prayer meetings held in the home of a Mrs. Brown by R.W.H. Hill, a merchant from Huntsville, Alabama.

Jonesboro United Methodist

On October 20, 1825, the second session of the Holston Annual Conference met here. Soon after this, the church built a small brick building on the southeastern edge of the town with rough slabs for seats and a brick floor. The fifth session of the Holston Conference met in that church in 1828.

The present Greek Revival building was completed in 1847, and the choir loft, pews, and windows were added at a later date. In 1875 the steeple was remodeled and the bell, cast in Cincinnati in 1866, was installed. The crystal chandelier from Czechoslovakia, created before World War II, was placed in the sanctuary in 1948.

The "Sister's Row" Building, built in 1820, owned by Jonesboro Methodist Church, has been refurbished and used for both religious and civic occasions. This long, two- storied, three-apartment building was built by Samuel D. Jackson in 1820 for his three daughters, and is perhaps the oldest building in Jonesboro.

Old Kingsport Presbyterian

Photo courtesy Karina McDaniel

Old Kingsport Presbyterian Church
Kingsport

A Kingsport group known as the Boatyard Congregation began worshipping in a log building; in 1820, permission was sought and granted to organize as a Presbyterian church. That same year an organizational meeting was presided over by Reverend James Gallaher, who later became Chaplain of the United States House of Representatives. The original congregation included both Black and White members.

In 1846, a new building was erected on property of Pastor Frederick Ross at his expense, using slaves. He deeded this property to the trustees of the church "for as long as the Kings Port Church remained in the new school of Presbyterians, U.S.A."

The church was not damaged during the Civil War, although the logs from the original building were used by the Federal army to build a bridge. The newly built railroad took business from the river port nearby. Membership dwindled, and efforts to revitalize the church met with little success.

In 1937, members and friends of the church came together in a meeting moderated by Reverend Hugh F. Ash to reorganize the congregation. The building was improved and a decision was made to remove the church from the railroad tracks to a better location. The move was made in 1953 to a site donated by Mrs. Octavia Patton. Today Old Kingsport Presbyterian is again an active church.

First Presbyterian, Kingsport

First United Methodist, Kingsport

First Baptist, Kingsport

Broad Street United Methodist, Kingsport

Church Circle District
Kingsport

The Church Circle is a small and beautifully maintained park surrounded by four handsome churches of Colonial Revival style. First Baptist, First United Methodist, First Presbyterian, and Broad Street United Methodist Churches, all built within the same time period and in accordance with the special design for Kingsport, have been a focal point of the city since their beginnings.

The Church Circle was created in the overall plan of a new industrial city between 1905 and 1909.

The First Methodist and Broad Street congregations have merged, and the First Methodist building is now the Kingsport Fine Arts Center.

Bethel Presbyterian Church
Kingston

Bethel Presbyterian Church is believed to have been organized in 1818 in Kingston, the third oldest town in Tennessee. Early records are scarce, but one original roll book, containing names of members, baptisms of children, and minutes of session meetings, is kept in a vault in the Kingston Bank and Trust Company.

The Reverend Isaac Anderson wrote in his personal records that he and a Mr. Morrison "held a service at Kingston, administering the sacrament, and organizing a church called Bethel in 1818." The first worship services of this church were held in the Rittenhouse Academy, a log building located on a hill sometimes called "Presbyterian Hill." There were both Black and White members in this early group; John Eagleton was chosen as the first pastor.

It is believed that John Riley, a Cherokee Indian, gave land for a cemetery and school nearby so that his children could attend school there.

A brick building was erected on the hill about 1920. It was replaced in 1858 by a white frame church, which was moved to its present location about 1883.

In 1868 a bell weighing two hundred and fifty pounds was donated by lawyers and clerks who had offices in the Roane County Courthouse. The bell is still in use.

Bethel Presbyterian, Kingston

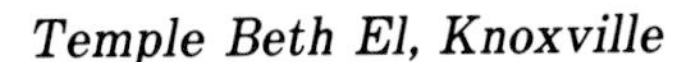

Temple Beth El, Knoxville

Temple Beth El
Knoxville

The first Jewish congregation in Knoxville was founded by the Hebrew Benevolent Association in 1864. The association had a threefold purpose: to provide proper religious services, to maintain a Jewish cemetery, and to collect funds for indigent and distressed Jews.

Early Knoxville Jews were highly respected, and many Christians attended special holiday services with them. One prominent early Jewish leader, Julius Ochs, was lay-rabbi, teacher, merchant, justice of the peace, fire insurance agent, United States commissioner, theater manager, and president of the German Association.

In 1914, the group found itself in need of a permanent house of worship, and the Congregational Church building at the corner of Broadway and West Vine Avenue, which had been abandoned, was acquired. It was dedicated on September 20, 1914, with Rabbi George Zepin of Cincinnati, Ohio, presiding. Rabbi Jerome Mark was installed in the presence of local members of his congregation and those from Athens, Harriman, Lenoir City, Jellico, Rockwood, and other towns in the area.

In 1954, property on Kingston Pike was purchased and the first synagogue built for that purpose in Knoxville was erected. This much-admired building, with stained glass by A. Raymond Katz, has been featured in an architectural exhibition in London.

First Baptist Church
Knoxville

On January 15, 1843, a group of prospective members met in an upper room in the Knox County courthouse and organized the Knoxville Baptist church. Twelve charter members invited Elder J.A. Bullock to become pastor for one year.

A simple building was erected, which was severely damaged during the Civil War; years later the Federal government reimbursed the congregation with $1200 for repairs to the building.

In 1868, Reverend D. M. Breaker became pastor and lived in the basement of the church. In June of that year, Captain W. W. Woodruff and his mother, Mrs. Ella T. Woodruff, became members of this church and remained active until their deaths. The Captain was soon the clerk of the church and later served as deacon for fifty-six years. When the second sanctuary was built, Woodruff matched every dollar donated by the entire membership for the building fund. He became the leader in the reorganization of the Baptist denomination in Knoxville after the Civil War.

First Baptist, Knoxville

Saint John's Lutheran Church
Knoxville

Saint John's Lutheran is a fine example of early twentieth century Gothic Revival church architecture. It was designed and built in 1913 by Knoxville architect Richard Franklin Graf, and retains its original integrity except for an addition at the rear in 1968.

Saint John's Evangelical Lutheran congregation was organized in 1888 by a group of former members of the German Lutheran Church, which had been founded in Knoxville in 1845. Originally known as the English Lutheran Church, the group worshipped in the German Lutheran Church on Sunday evenings. In 1892, the new congregation purchased the Broad Street Methodist Church, where they worshipped until 1910. That building no longer stands.

Two lots on Broadway at Emory Place were purchased in 1910, and ground was broken for the present church of Gothic Revival architecture on August 11, 1911. Built of gray rusticated stone with Gothic stained glass windows, buttresses, and corner towers, the church was dedicated on May 25, 1913.

Outstanding features of the interior are five stained glass windows with dark stained surrounds, ogee moldings, and the original pulpit and pews. The dominant interior feature is the dark oak hammer beam trusswork supporting the grooved panel ceiling.

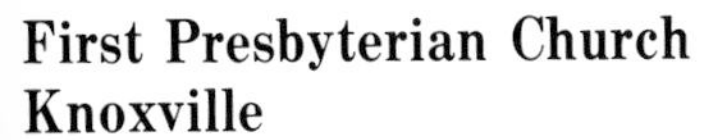

Saint John's Lutheran, Knoxville

First Presbyterian, Knoxville

First Presbyterian Church Knoxville

Captain James White of Iredell, North Carolina, arrrived in what is now Knoxville in 1786, and settled on a site near the river with four other families. Charles McClung, a surveyor, laid out sixty-four half-acre lots which sold for eight dollars each. On a lot reserved for Captain White, he designated a section for the site of a church and a cemetery.

No deed has been found for the church lot, although the first church in Knoxville was built on it. A church was active in this town as early as 1793, but the courthouse served as the meeting place until the first church was completed in 1816. It was used until 1852.

Samuel Carrick, one of the original settlers in Captain White's party, became the first pastor and continued to serve until his death in 1809.

In 1856, a new and larger building was constructed covering part of the site of the old building, and a part of the cemetery was enclosed within the wall of the building. A door from the lecture room gives access to that part of the basement, and a plaque on the north side of the church shows the names of those graves enclosed.

During the Civil War, the church and cemetery were used as barracks, hospital, Freedman's School, and much damage was done, but by 1871, under the leadership of Pastor James Park, restoration had been significant.

In 1903 a new and more modern church of Greek Revival architecture was built slightly to the north of the original. The building was enlarged and remodeled when the wings were added in 1924-25.

The earliest date on a headstone in the cemetery is 1800. In 1857 a city ordinance was passed forbidding further burials.

Church of the Immaculate Conception, Catholic Knoxville

Father Stephen Theodore Badin of Bardstown, Kentucky, visited Knoxville and organized a Catholic congregation in 1809. No house of worship was built in Knoxville until 1852, when the present building of Romanesque architecture was constructed.

Saint Mary's Parochial School, staffed by the Sisters of Charity of Nazareth, Kentucky, was opened here during the Civil War.

At the close of the war, Father Abram J. Ryan, the "Poet Priest of the South" who had spent the war years as a chaplain in the Confederate army, became priest of this church. The original manuscript of his well-known "The Conquered Banner" is in the possession of a Knoxville family.

In 1908, Holy Ghost Church was established and Holy Ghost School opened, staffed by the Sisters of Mercy. In 1918, Knoxville Catholic High School was opened on Magnolia Avenue, and in 1928 Saint Mary's Memorial Hospital was established on Oak Street.

Church of the Immaculate Conception, Knoxville

First Christian, Knoxville

Church Street Methodist, Knoxville

Church Street Methodist Church Knoxville

This church of Gothic Revival Architecture is built of stone and has been a landmark in Knoxville for decades.

Knoxville was first mentioned as a "preaching place" in records of the Conference at Fountain Head, Middle Tennessee, on November 12, 1812, with Samuel H. Thompson in charge.

In 1815 a small frame building was erected for the Methodist group on Methodist Hill. John Haynie was in charge of building that church in 1834. This new church was referred to in later years as the "Old Methodist Church."

During the Civil War, few if any worship services were held. The Union army occupied the city and used all available buildings.

The Methodist Church was reorganized in 1866. The "Old Methodist Church" on Church Street was taken by the northern church; the Methodist Episcopal Church, South, worshipped in the basement of First Presbyterian Church until 1867, when they built a new brick chapel.

In 1875, the Southern denomination reclaimed the old church and the lot on which it stood and built a brick church there. It was dedicated in February 1878 by Bishop Wrightman and Dr. R. A. Young.

Saint John's Episcopal, Knoxville

First Christian Church
Knoxville

First Christian Church was organized with seventeen members on September 6, 1874, in an upper room at the corner of Depot and Broad Streets. Soon a "meeting house" was built on McGhee Street, and in 1886 a church was built at the corner of Park and Gay Streets. The congregation then adopted the name Park Avenue Christian Church.

The third pastor of this congregation, Ashley S. Johnson, established Johnson Bible College in Knox County in 1887. This school is still active in preparing ministers for the Christian Church.

The present Greek Revival church was built in 1915 by Barber and McMurry, architects. This impressive building features a tile roof and arched windows, a trademark of Barber and McMurry. First Christian Church was the focal point of a 1975 exhibit of "Lost Knoxville and Architecture Worth Saving in Knoxville" at the Dulin Gallery.

The name of the church became Fifth Avenue Christian when the present building was erected, and was changed to First Christian in May 1926.

Saint John's Protestant Episcopal Church
Knoxville

The Reverend Thomas W. Humes, a Suffragan Bishop in the Diocese of Tennessee and later President of the University of Tennesssee, has been called "the father of Saint John's Church." A long-time Presbyterian who had once hoped to become a minister, Humes had attended the Theological Seminary of Princeton University. He abandoned his ambition after one year and returned to Knoxville, where he established a mercantile business.

Later Humes did become a candidate for the ministry, this time in the Episcopal Church. Reverend James Otey appointed him a lay leader, and he became active in that role.

When Saint John's was organized on May 9, 1844, there was only one confirmed communicant in Knoxville. Worship was held in the home of Humes' brother-in-law, H.A.M. White, located where the University of Tennessee School of Home Economics now stands. Later Humes' brother provided a small building at the corner of Gay and Church Streets, which was used for two years.

On his first visit to this church in 1845, Bishop Otey laid the cornerstone for a new church at the corner of Cumberland and Walnut Street, where it stood until the present stone building of Romanesque architecture replaced it in 1892. Reverend Charles Tomes of New York was appointed by Bishop Otey to serve as minister of Saint John's. Soon he married Bishop Otey's daughter and became Rector of Christ Church, Nashville, where he served many years.

In 1873, Saint John's founded the Saint John's Orphanage, later named Children's Episcopal Home, where children of all faiths and those whose families have no church affiliation are served.

Broadway Baptist Church
Knoxville

Broadway Baptist Church began as a mission Sunday School of First Baptist Church. Started in a rented building on the corner of Broad and Depot Streets, this church complex now encompasses two city blocks bounded by Broadway, Irwin, Bearden Place, and Gill Streets.

Two lots in the Dameron Addition of Knoxville were donated by W.W. Woodruff, a deacon in First Baptist Church, for establishing a second Baptist church. That building, called Calvary Chapel, was completed in February 1882. Calvary Baptist Church was organized there in 1885 under the guidance of Dr. O.L. Hailey, a missionary of the State Mission Board. Soon additional property was acquired at the corner of Broad and Walnut Streets and a church building was begun in 1889.

The congregation, then known as Second Baptist Church, worshipped in the basement of the building for nine years until the sanctuary was completed. On October 1, an estimated fifteen hundred people attended the dedication service.

On Christmas Eve, 1965, a fire set by arsonists destroyed the sanctuary and educational building. While the fire raged, the pastor, Dr. Lewis Rhodes, gathered two hundred members in the parking lot, and together they decided to hold worship on Sunday, December 26. Members and friends of the church worked all Christmas Day enclosing the parking garage, where an estimated one thousand people gathered to worship on the day after Christmas.

The present church of Neoclassical design with a free-standing bell tower was dedicated on Easter Sunday, April 14, 1968. On that day, the congregation gathered again in the parking garage, and, after prayers, marched together into the new sanctuary.

Broadway Baptist, Knoxville

Shannondale Presbyterian Church
Knoxville

This church was organized on Tazewell Pike in 1802 by William Shannon Anderson and John A. McCampbell, who donated land for a church site. Plans for the building were drawn by Stephenson and Getz, Knoxville architects and builders, and Mr. L.A. Galyon served as building contractor.

Stained glass windows, considered treasures, were given by Second Presbyterian Church of Knoxville, with surplus ones stored in the barn of James A. Anderson. Some time later the barn burned and the windows were destroyed.

The old communion service is prized possession of this congregation.

"Lebanon-in-the-Forks" Presbyterian
Knoxville

"Lebanon-in-the-Forks" was the first Presbyterian church organized in what is now Knox County. Reverend Samuel Carrick established the church in 1791, assisted by a board of elders which included Captain James White, the founder of Knoxville.

The first building, made of unhewn logs, was twenty feet square and had a dirt floor. In 1793 a new building of hewn logs was constructed on land donated by Colonel F. A. Ramsey; it measured forty by sixty feet and had a floor and pews. This structure was replaced in 1808 by a small stone church, which was in turn replaced by a larger and more appropriate stone building in 1848. The present Greek Revival church, built in 1902, has two front doors in an unusual configuration.

The list of early ministers includes Reverend Samuel Carrick, founder of Blount College, which became the University of Tennessee; Reverend Isaac Anderson; and Reverend Hezekiah Balch, founder of Greeneville College. The nearby cemetery contains headstones of many prominent people, including Carrick and Dr. J.G.M. Ramsey.

Lebanon-in-the-Forks Presbyterian, Knoxville

hannondale Presbyterian, Knoxville

nmanuel Episcopal Church a Grange

his brick church with stuccoed front features a abled roof, handsome Gothic detailing, and fine oodwork. The lancet windows and the pews are plicas of the originals; the original pews were used r the coffins of Union soldiers during the Civil ar.

This congregation was organized and the church uilt as a result of efforts of Mrs. Mary Hayes loster, who rode on horseback from La Grange to ranklin in 1832 to seek help from her godson, ishop James Hervey Otey. She had settled in La range with family and acquaintances, and was nhappy that there was no Episcopal church in the nmediate area.

For what is referred to as "Mrs. Gloster's horse de," she carried her one-year-old grandchild and a g of peach brandy made from her own recipe. rriving in Franklin, she explained the situation to ishop Otey and received an immediate and vorable response. Reverend Thomas Wright was nt to West Tennessee, where he organized five urches within a few months. Immanuel was the rst Episcopal church organized west of the ennessee River.

Mrs. Gloster's slaves are said to have made the ick and built the church, which is a replica of the urch in which she had worshipped in North arolina for many years. It was consecrated in 1843. disastrous storm in 1900 destroyed the other urches in La Grange, but Immanuel Church was ared.

Immanuel Episcopal, LaGrange

Sacred Heart of Jesus, Lawrenceburg

Sacred Heart of Jesus, Catholic
Lawrenceburg

In the winter of 1869-70, representatives of the Cincinnati German Catholic Homestead Society visited Lawrence County. The purpose of the visit was to locate and purchase land for resettlement of German Catholics in the Ohio Valley, who were suffering from the financial depression which followed the Civil War.

By 1870, fifteen thousand acres had been purchased to the north and west of Lawrenceburg through the efforts of Reverend Henry Huesser, pastor of a church in Cincinnati, who had stayed in Tennessee for that purpose. Settlers began arriving, and soon fifty German and Polish families were settled in the area. Few had experience as farmers.

Mass was first celebrated in Lawrenceburg on October 24, 1870, by Father Huesser, in an old home on Fain Street. A wooden frame church building was built in 1872 at Groh Street and Buffalo Road, and the Fathers of the Precious Blood were soon settled in a farmhouse.

A convent and school were soon established, and work was begun in 1886 on the present church building, which was consecrated by Bishop Joseph Rademacher in 1890. The present rectory on the same grounds was completed in the same year.

One of four German Catholic Churches built in the latter part of the nineteenth century in Lawrence County, Sacred Heart of Jesus remains the only one still active. Architecturally, it presents an Upper Rhine Valley air and is a prominent landmark in the county.

Quarter-sawed oak pews are original, and colorful stencilling on the walls and ceiling in the nave and apse is noteworthy. The unusual ceramic Stations of the Cross are also among the treasures of this church.

Sister Juliana, Administrator of St. Thomas Hospital in Nashville, whose ancestors were early members of this church, was baptized and confirmed here.

James Daniel Niedergeses, Bishop of the Diocese of Tennessee, was also a member of Sacred Heart of Jesus Church, and stated that his grandfather hewed the timbers for the steeple on the building. His father and other children in the church school carved the beautiful reredos behind the altar.

First Presbyterian Church
Lebanon

The cornerstone of First Presbyterian Church was laid on August 10, 1910, with Dr. S. A. Coile, pastor, and Judge Nathan Green officiating. The site for this Gothic Revival brick church was purchased from D. W. Braden and R. V. and Bell Braden Foster. The church was dedicated in September 1911.

A wealth of stained glass is a feature of the sanctuary, where an unusual cross graces the altar. In 1960 additional space and a chapel were completed.

Among the community services here are a nursery school and activities for senior and underprivileged citizens.

First Presbyterian, Lebanon

First Methodist, Lebanon

First United Methodist Church
Lebanon

A small group of Methodists began worshipping under a brush arbor about 1800. In bad weather they held their services in the small Wilson County courthouse on the Public Square.

In 1829, the Methodist group paid seventy-five dollars for a building lot and erected a building measuring forty by sixty feet. This was the first church in Lebanon. They shared the church with the Cumberland Presbyterian worshippers, who had outgrown the space in the courthouse.

The church, still standing, was made of handmade brick with walls sixteen inches thick. The belfry contains a bell dating from early times; a slave gallery at the rear of the building has been removed. The last conference attended by Bishop McKendree was held in this building in 1834.

The building has been preserved and is now the property of Virginia Lawlor, third great-granddaughter of Edward Morris, one of the builders and first trustees of the church.

The present church of Classical architecture stands on West Main Street.

Liberty United Methodist, Liberty

South Harpeth Church of Christ, Linton

South Harpeth Church of Christ
Linton

On May 12, 1812, Joseph Davey donated one acre for the purpose of building "a meeting house and burial ground." This is the oldest Church of Christ in Davidson County and one of the oldest in the nation.

The first log building on this site burned and was replaced by a wooden frame church, which burned about 1840. The present church was built in 1845 of handmade brick; the nearby cemetery was enclosed in a stone wall at about the same time.

In 1950, Mrs. Bettie Allen, who owned property between the church and the new highway and held reserve on the old church, released the church site and donated land on which a new church was built.

Among the early ministers at South Harpeth Church were Talbot Fanning, William Anderson, E. J. Sewell, J.C. McQuiddy, James A. Harding, and David Lipscomb.

Liberty United Methodist Church
DeKalb County

Founded in 1800, the Liberty Methodist congregation worshipped in homes of the members until 1825, when a church was erected on one fourth acre of land deeded to Methodists and Presbyterians by Adam Dale, the first settler in the area. The two-storied building had a large opening over the pulpit so that slaves sitting in the upper room could look down upon the minister.

During the Civil War, Black soldiers were quartered in the church. When the war was over it became a barn, sheltering both cattle and hogs. Finally it was restored, and worship services were held there until 1874, when the present building of Victorian Gothic architecture was erected.

On October 19, 1939, the Presbyterian congregation ceded their rights to the property to the Methodist congregation.

First United Methodist Church Livingston

This congregation was called Mountain Mission when it was organized in 1834, but at the Annual Conference meeting in Columbia in 1836, the name was changed to Livingston Mission in honor of the Honorable Edward Livingston, who later became Secretary of State. The original membership included 765 White members and 69 Black members.

Mrs. Minerva Phillips Stover, wife of Hiram Stover and daughter of Mr. and Mrs. Beaty Phillips, stated that she baked and brought to Livingston Mission the first bread used in Livingston for sacramental purposes in 1838.

Worship was suspended during the Civil War, and reconstruction of the church was difficult. The Cumberland Presbyterian congregation built a comfortable building after the war and invited the Methodist congregation to worship with them, a gesture which they accepted. This building, which burned in 1888, was used as the Overton County courthouse from 1864 to 1870, when a new courthouse was erected.

In 1868, Sheriff John Boles of Overton County called Governor William G. Brownlow for help from the state militia to suppress action by the Ku Klux Klan attempting to control "carpetbaggers." The milita arrived, organized in Jamestown, camped at Cave Springs, and some of them took up quarters in the Cumberland Presbyterian Church in Livingston. While they were there an epidemic of measles swept through the area and several of the men died there. They are buried in the Cash Cemetery.

Efforts of Lloyd Chafin started a movement in 1888 to build a Methodist church, and in 1891 a frame building was dedicated. Yellow poplar siding, painted white, was the distinguishing feature of this small church at the corner of North Church and Henson Streets.

Tom Sexton, noted blacksmith preacher, preached here.

In 1954, the building was sold and a lot was purchased at the corner of Roberts and Main Streets. John Charles Wheeler of Nashville, architect, designed the present Greek Revival style church and J. B. Copeland served as supervisor of the project. The cornerstone was laid July 22, 1958, and the first worship service was held March 15, 1959.

First United Methodist, Livingston

Sacred Heart of Jesus Catholic Church Loretto

In 1871, Father Henry Huesser relocated from Lawrenceburg to Loretto, where a wooden building which served as a church and a school was erected.

Built in 1911, the present small brick church combines features of Victorian Gothic and Romanesque Revival architecture. It has a bell tower and stepped brick corner buttresses, and is decorated with a dogtooth course of brick encircling the building and on the bell tower. Interesting stained glass windows remain in place.

German Catholic settlements and churches were originally established at Saint Joseph, at Saint Mary's, here, and in Lawrenceburg. All that remains of Saint Mary's is a cemetery, five miles from the village of Saint Joseph. Only Sacred Heart of Jesus Church in Lawrenceburg is still active.

Sacred Heart of Jesus, Loretto

Cumberland Presbyterian of Loudon
Loudon

Cumberland Presbyterian Church, located on College Street, is a fine example of Victorian Gothic architecture This wood building of batten and board construction features distinct Gothic influence in lancet-arch windows set in pointed-arch frames, steep gables and wood-bracket trim at the eaves.

The congregation was organized in 1853 and occupied a building on Church Street, which was taken over by Federal troops for use as a hospital. At the close of the war, Cumberland Presbyterian Church reclaimed their building and worshipped there until 1877, when it was sold to the Loudon School Commission, which in turn sold it to the Presbyterian Church; it was demolished in 1916.

The Cumberland Presbyterians began to worship with the Methodist congregation, and continued to do so until their present building was finished in 1882. The builder of this church was J. M. "Boss" Clark, a well-known contractor in the area.

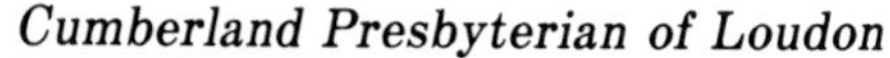

Cumberland Presbyterian of Loudon

Saint Paul's Presbyterian, Lowland

Saint Paul's Presbyterian Church
Lowland

Standing on a gentle rise five and a half miles southeast of the Hamblen county courthouse, the present rectangular brick church replaced a stone building which is believed to have been the first Presbyterian Church in the county. It was organized in 1804 by settlers of the "Bend of Chuckey" section of Jefferson County (now Hamblen County).

This small Greek Revival building is made of brick laid in stretcher bond and was completed in 1857 under the supervision of Colonel Joseph Hamilton, a prominent member of the church. John Seaholt, a Dandridge contractor, was awarded the contract for the construction, and William A. Stover did the woodwork. Reverend William Harvey Smith preached the first sermon in the new church in January 1858. This church is a good example of rural East Tennessee Greek Revival churches of the mid-nineteenth century. The exterior of the church retains its original architectural integrity. When more floor space was necessary, the congregation voted to excavate and construct rooms in the basement rather than add wings to the sides of the building.

A three acre cemetery on the church grounds dates to 1859.

Madison Church of Christ, Madison

City Road United Methodist Church
Madison

A Methodist chapel was erected at the present site in 1850, and it is believed that a church had been organized here earlier. A deed to the property was recorded November 22, 1850, by the trustees of the site. The first building lasted twenty years.

On August 5, 1871, City Road Chapel and McFerrin's Chapel, named in honor of John B. McFerrin, united and took the name Midway. They located a place of worship halfway between the two former churches. The Quarterly Conference met at Midway in May 1872 and again February 1899. The church burned in May 1899.

With Reverend John B. McFerrin as pastor, it was agreed that a new church should be built at the present site, and on September 3, 1899, the cornerstone of this Romanesque stone church was laid and the name became City Road Chapel.

The first church of John Wesley in London was called City Road Chapel and is known as the shrine of world Methodism.

The dedication sermon was given September 1, 1901, by Dr. W. F. Tillett, Dean of the School of Religion, Vanderbilt University. City Road Chapel became a station in 1929, with Reverend Boyd S. Fielder as first pastor.

City Road United Methodist, Madison

Madison Church of Christ
Madison

During the Thanksgiving season in 1934, seven people met in the home of Mrs. Granville L. Campbell and made plans for organizing a Church of Christ in Madison when a meeting place could be located.

Duncan's Garage on Main Street, being vacant at the time, was rented by the group. After greasy floors and dirty windows were cleaned, a crude pulpit constructed, stoves donated, songbooks and a communion table borrowed, the first worship service of the congregation was held by Price Billingsley. There were 110 persons present.

The congregation is now worshipping in its third building, where thousands of people are in attendance each Sunday. Many more participate in its numerous and varied programs of religious and community service.

Reverend Ira L. North, pastor here for thirty-two years, was a respected leader in both religious and civic causes in Madison and Nashville.

Madison Church of Christ now has more than four thousand members, making it the largest Church of Christ congregation in the world.

First Baptist Church
Madisonville

Tellico Baptist Church was organized in 1828, and became a regular church on March 3, 1828, with Elder George Snider and Daniel Buckner presiding. There were twenty-one charter members, and Snider and Buckner served as co-pastors until 1833.

The name of the village was changed from Tellico to Madisonville in 1845, when it became the county seat of Monroe County.

The first log church burned in 1858. It was replaced with a frame building which was used until 1924, when the present neo-classical building was completed.

Dr. H. F. Buckner, a member of this church, worked as a missionary to the Creek Indians for thirty-five years, and the Reverend David B. Kimbrough served as a Tennessee Baptist Convention missionary from 1873 to 1875.

Among the many pastors who served here was Reverend Jacob Peter Kefauver, great-grandfather of Estes Kefauver, United States Senator from Tennessee.

First Baptist, Madisonville

Martel United Methodist

Martel United Methodist Church
Martel

This church, known historically as Muddy Creek Methodist Church, traces its history to the early days of Methodism in Tennessee.

Sometime before 1795, the Reverend John Winton came to Muddy Creek in Loudon County and established a seat of worship. Undoubtedly he preached in a log building. Bishop Francis Asbury, whose circuit extended from New York to Charleston, South Carolina, visited Muddy Creek Church many times. Along with Bishop Whatcoat and Bishop McKendree, he visited this church on October 31, 1800, and together they ordained John Winton as a deacon.

Winton conducted camp meetings here for many years, and in 1843 deeded the camp ground and everything thereon to the Methodist Church. He died in 1846 and is buried in the nearby cemetery.

Before the Civil War another log church was built at Muddy Creek. It contained a gallery for slaves and stood until General Burnsides, on his way through the area, ordered his men to dismantle the church and nearby cabins and remove them to Ball Camp Ground in Knox County.

Undaunted, the members of Muddy Creek Church hauled lumber and built a platform under a large oak tree. Worship services were held with a minister preaching from the platform to a congregtation standing on the ground below.

Soon a new building was begun, with members contributing whatever they could. One donor was a Colonel Easley, a Presbyterian minister, who contributed to the building in return for the privilege of having a Presbyterian minister preach there once a month.

The present church was dedicated in 1872, and the name changed to Martel in 1939.

First United Methodist Church
Martin

Organized in 1873 with twenty-seven charter members, this congregation began worshipping in a one room frame building in 1876. This property was later sold to the Cumberland Presbyterian church, and the Methodist congregation moved across the street.

The present church with two spires was built in 1896 on the same site. A parsonage was built opposite the church on a lot where the first house in Martin had stood. An educational annex was built on this lot in 1922, and in 1934 the original parsonage was replaced by a brick cottage.

In 1952, Clarence and George Dodd bought the Bruce Hotel west of the annex and donated it to the church to remodel for a youth center. Robert Harrison was the architect for this project. The building is used as a community center as well as a church facility.

First Methodist, Martin

Zion Presbyterian, Maury County

Zion Presbyterian Church
Maury County

Between 1805 and 1808, Scotch-Irish settlers arrived in Maury County from South Carolina. Among them were descendants of John Knox, who organized and built a log church in August 1807 before they built homes for their families.

The church stood near the center of a 5,120 acre tract of land purchased from heirs of General Nathaniel Greene, who had received 25,000 acres for his service in the Revolutionary War. This log building was used for worship for six years and replaced by a small brick one.

The present church, completed in 1849, was built by members and slaves who halved timbers and burned the bricks at the site. It measures eighty by fifty feet and is three stories high. Built in Greek Revival style, it features a recessed porch. A school which James K. Polk attended was conducted by the church.

Sunday School was held here as early as 1810, and Black members were in Sunday School in 1867. One hundred and forty-five Black members were listed on the membership rolls that year.

The unique custom of using communion tokens was discontinued here in 1833. Scotch-Irish Presbyterians had long issued tokens to members who had received communion on Saturday before Sacrament Sunday. Some of these lead tokens marked "ZC," a chair, a Bible, a psalter used by Reverend James White Stephenson, a pewter communion service, old blue communion plates, and a diorama depicting the early history of Zion Church are among the relics here.

An old cemetery lies nearby, where amid the boxwood shrubs and giant trees are found graves of fifteen Revolutionary War soldiers, three from the War of 1812, one from the Seminole War of 1836, sixty Confederate soldiers, and others from later wars, along with thirteen ministers and their wives.

Hopewell Presbyterian, Maury County

New Providence Presbyterian, Maryville

Hopewell Presbyterian Church
Maury County

Organized in 1806 by Reverend Duncan Brown, who came to Middle Tennessee from North Carolina, New Hope Church was founded by settlers of Scottish and Irish descent who were faithful to strict religious law. The first house of worship here was built on land granted to them by the State of North Carolina for service in the Revolutionary War.

The present white clapboard church, standing in a grove of trees, was built in 1869 and provided separate doors and pews for men and women. A partition through the center of the sanctuary was sufficiently high to prevent the men and women, boys and girls, from seeing each other above it. This partition was removed in 1970, but notches where the partition was fastened to the pews can still be seen.

New Providence Presbyterian Church
Maryville

The first New Providence Church was built in 1792 by Reverend Gideon Blackburn, who arrived at Fort Craig with a Bible and a rifle protected by a company of militia from Jefferson County. Serving as

pastor of this church and also of Eusebia Church, he often held joint meetings at a campground on an island in Little River near Brabson's Ford.

In 1802, Gideon Blackburn became the first missionary to the Cherokee Indians from the Presbyterian General Assembly. He resigned from the two churches in 1810 and was succeeded by Reverend Isaac Anderson in 1812. Anderson served forty-five years.

The log church in which New Providence had worshipped since the beginning was replaced in 1829 by a stone building containing galleries on three sides. This building was small, and on occasion worship services took place on a campground nearby. Complete records were not kept until 1840, but in that year Joseph Hart recorded a membership of six hundred members, and then added "after the purge," three hundred members.

In 1852, the stone church was torn down and another built on the same site. Some of the stones were used in a wall around the cemetery at Cates and Broadway, where the first three buildings stood.

The next building was somewhat sub-standard, and the congregation was displeased with it; it was further damaged during the Civil War. In 1890, a new church was built at College Street and Broadway. The present building, constructed of native stone in Gothic design, was completed in 1953.

Eusebia Presbyterian Church
Maryville

In the summer of 1786, Reverend Archibald Scott arrived in Tennessee from Augusta County, Virginia. In the wilderness of what later became Blount County, he established two Presbyterian churches: Eusebia, at McTeer's Fort, and New Providence at Craig's Fort.

It was at a camping ground long used by early travelers that Eusebia was located, beneath a large beech tree near a spring. According to local tradition, a woman of an early immigrant party died in the place and was buried in a crude coffin made from wagon boards. An early tombstone bore the date 1790 and the name Joseph Bogle.

In 1792, Gideon Blackburn arrived at Fort Craig from Jefferson County and built a church. In 1794, he became pastor of Eusebia and New Providence Churches. In 1797, Eusebia reported forty families and was able to pay a pastor $130 per year. Soon the old log church was replaced with a large frame building, which featured a pulpit four feet high with steps on each side with elaborate railings. A small brick church replaced that frame building in 1874. The present church was built in 1930.

This church has had many pastors who were students at Maryville College, a Presbyterian institution nearby. According to Union Presbytery records, Dr. Alexander McGhee, described as a converted atheist, was ordained and served as pastor from 1824 until 1927.

The old cemetery is the burial ground for many Revolutionary soldiers and some Indians. Early graves of settlers murdered by Indians have been marked by the Mary Blount Chapter, Daughters of the American Revolution.

Baker's Creek Presbyterian Church
Maryville

Reverend Gideon Blackburn organized this church in 1796 and served as the first pastor. It is one of the original churches established by this noted churchman, who began preaching at the nearby New Providence and Eusebia churches in 1792 at age twenty.

Located in the heart of Tennessee Presbyterianism, Baker's Creek Church has long been involved in denominational activity. The Holston Presbytery was reorganized after the Civil War at Baker's Creek on August 23, 1866.

A nearby cemetery contains the graves of many early settlers and prominent people of the area, including Elizabeth Paxton Houston, mother of Sam Houston.

Eusebia Presbyterian, Maryville

Baker's Creek Presbyterian, Maryville

Central Church of Christ, McMinnville

Central Church of Christ McMinnville

As early as 1830, a group of Church of Christ members was worshipping in the Warren County courthouse. Soon after 1840, Brother Sandy E. Jones preached the first sermon to this group in a small brick church of their own.

The building was abused and deteriorated during the Civil War, but was repaired and used for worship until 1878, when another one was erected. In 1877, H. L. Walling began raising funds for that new church. He and his brother Jesse and W. P. Faulkner subscribed fifty per cent of the necessary amount.

The present Greek Revival church has a seating capacity of one thousand and was completed in October 1973.

First United Methodist Church McMinnville

Records do not reveal the date of organization of this church, but the name appears as host of the Second Quarterly Conference in 1836. In 1844, membership was listed as 31 white and 49 Black members.

In 1847, the Quarterly Conference appointed a committee to supervise the building of a meeting house for this group in McMinnville. There were various delays, and in 1851 another committee was appointed.

A small building was erected at the rear of Magness Memorial Library and Community House. It was in use until 1888, when it was sold and the present Gothic church was erected.

After thirty years, a lot at the rear of the sanctuary was purchased, and an educational building was erected. This was made possible by a gift to the church in the will of Colonel John L. Willis, well-known attorney and trustee of the church for many years.

First United Methodist, McMinnville

Shiloh Cumberland Presbyterian, McKenzie

Shiloh Cumberland Presbyterian Church McKenzie

A group met at the home of Thomas Hamilton in Carroll County on October 19, 1825, and recessed to meet the next day in the Shiloh Meeting House. Tradition says that this Meeting House was erected in 1823 but no record has been found to verify this. The Reverend John H. Smith was probably the first pastor, and his gravestone in the Shiloh Cemetery marks his death as March 16, 1830.

Thomas Hamilton, in his autobiography written when he was eighty years old, tells the story of his conversion in a camp meeting at Little Muddy River in Fulton County, Kentucky, in 1800. Uniting with the Ridge Church near his father's home, he was ordained as Ruling Elder of this group in 1809. This church with the entire congregation became a part of the Cumberland Presbyterian Church on February 4, 1810.

Hamilton had fought under General Carroll during the war of 1812, and moved to the Shiloh Community in Carroll County in 1822. Here he became active in the Shiloh Church and died here in 1879 at the age of ninety. He is buried in the Shiloh Cemetery.

The original church was built of logs and was soon outgrown. The second building was also too small for the growing congregation, and a third was built after the Civil War.

This church, made of clapboard and designed for long range needs, had a high partition to separate the pews, thereby separating the men from the women. A gallery across one end was for the Black members of the congregation. A major renovation program including brick veneer was concluded in 1952.

Bellevue Baptist Church Memphis

In 1898, a mission of Central Baptist Church which later became Bellevue Baptist was started at Bellevue and Erskine Streets. With 16,000 members, it is now the largest church east of the Mississipi River and the second largest in the United States.

The mission was made possible by a gift of $1,000 provided in the will of Mrs. Fannie A. Jobe. Mr. Jesse Odell, chairman of a committee of three, rode a bicycle through the streets of Memphis to inspect the chosen site. Erskine Street was unpaved, had no sidewalks, and there were no houses in the area. The location was approved, and worship services were held there by the mission on Sunday afternoons until the summer of 1903, when it was dedicated as a church. Dr. H. P. Hurt became the first pastor.

A building, referred to as "the Little Stone Chapel," was erected at a cost of $12,000. The original name of the church was Bellevue Avenue Baptist Church, but the word "Avenue" was deleted later. When Dr. Hurt retired in 1914, membership had grown from thirty-two charter members to more than eight hundred.

In 1922 the "Little Stone Chapel" was razed and a new church was built. It was dedicated on March 19, 1924. Worship services were conducted in Tech High School on Poplar Street while the new church was being built.

In 1927, Dr. Robert Greene Lee became pastor of Bellevue Church, and served in this capacity for thirty-two years. Born in York County, South Carolina, on November 11, 1886, he came to Bellevue from Citadel Square Baptist Church in Charleston at age forty-one. While at Bellevue Church, Dr. Lee served three terms as president of the Southern Baptist Convention.

During his pastorate, Bellevue became the first church in the world to have a fully-equipped television studio. Much renovation was accomplished during that time; the old sanctuary was enlarged and later designated "Lee Auditorium." Indebtedness was fully paid, and in 1952 the present sanctuary was built.

Dr. Lee resigned as pastor but remained until 1960, when a new pastor was installed. During his years as pastor of this church, membership had grown from 1,430 to more than 9,000.

In 1960 Dr. Ramsey Pollard came to Bellevue Church as pastor from First Baptist Church in Knoxville, where he had served for twenty-one years. At that time he was president of the Southern Baptist Convention, and he was later elected to serve a second term in that post.

While Dr. Pollard was pastor, an activities building was completed at a cost of half a million dollars, a sanctuary and educational building were erected for Bellevue's mission church, City View, and color television was installed at Bellevue. The black and white television equipment was given to a church in Taiwan.

Bellevue Baptist's sixth pastor, Dr. Adrian Rogers, came to the church in 1972 from First Baptist Church, Merritt Island, Florida. He was elected president of the Pastor's Conference of the Southern Baptist Convention in 1975 and served as president of the Southern Baptist Convention in 1980 and again in 1986.

Bellevue Baptist, Memphis

Baron Hirsch Congregation
Memphis

Baron Maurice D. Hirsch, an Austrian Jewish capitalist and philanthropist, was born in Munich, Germany in 1831 and died in 1896. He was an international banker and builder of railroads, including the first railroad to connect Europe and Asia. His fortune was estimated at two hundred million dollars, nearly all of which he spent for the improvement of the condition of Jews around the world.

Baron Hirsch chartered ships, at his own expense, to remove Jews from Russia, and gave fifty million dollars to establish Jewish colonies in Argentina. In the United States his funds were used to Americanize, educate, and settle immigrants in many parts of the country. He was the benefactor of East European Jews who settled in Memphis between 1880 and 1890.

On June 4, 1892, the Baron Hirsch Benevolent Society was incorporated in Memphis. About the same time, the congregation purchased a church at the corner of Fourth and Washington Streets and converted it into a Synagogue. Much of the necessary repair work on the building was done by carpenters, roofers, and painters from within the congregation. In 1914, a new building was erected on this site.

On January 4, 1945, a resolution was passed to sell the property at Fourth and Washington Streets and build a new synagogue with an educational building. In 1945, land was purchased at Evergreen and Valentine Streets. Mr. George Awsumb was employed as architect in July 1946, and Philip Belz was retained as the builder of what would become the largest synagogue, for the largest congregation, in the world.

The cornerstone of the Baron Hirsch synagogue sanctuary was unveiled November 27, 1955. It is a block of Jerusalem marble brought from the Holy Land by Mr. and Mrs. Philip Belz. Rabbi and Mrs. Isadore Goodman brought a sack of earth from Mount Zion to be mixed with the mortar and cement to set the cornerstone in place.

This house of worship, a modern adaptation of Greek Revival architecture, stands on a fourteen-acre tract of land and measures 100 by 326 feet. The exterior walls are limestone, and the walks are Crab Orchard stone. Walls in the lobbies are white oak, and walls in other areas are Travertine marble.

The sanctuary floors are carpeted; other floors are terrazzo, and the walls are walnut and plaster. Arks in the sanctuary and chapel have bronze doors and symbolisms. Stained glass by Jack Gure, noted miniature artist, and by George Awsumb and sons, is featured throughout.

Baron Hirsch Congregation, Memphis

Clayborn Temple, Memphis

Clayborn Temple
Memphis

This monumental building of Romanesque Revival design was completed in October 1892 for the Second Presbyterian congregation, one of the first Black churches in Memphis. It was purchased fifty years later by the African Methodist Episcopal Church, which changed the name to Clayborn Temple.

The massive walls and tower are unusual in church architecture of the period and are considered rare in Memphis. The building was designed by Minneapolis architects Frederick Kees and Franklin B. Long, with Edward C. Jones of Memphis serving as supervising architect.

During the Memphis sanitation strike in April 1968, Dr. Martin Luther King, Jr., delivered the organizing speech in Clayborn Temple. He was assassinated on April 4 of that year in Memphis.

Clayborn Temple Coalition has been formed for the purpose of restoring this church and other landmarks in the area.

First United Methodist, Memphis

First United Methodist Church
Memphis

Groundbreaking ceremonies for this Victorian Gothic Revival church were held in May 1887, and the dedication was held in January 1893. Built of limestone from Alabama and ironstone from Arkansas, this building is the third erected for this congregation. Many alterations have been made to the interior, while the outer appearance remains much the same as it was in 1893.

Methodists were the first religious group to organize a church in Memphis, at a meeting of three people in the home of Reverend Thomas P. Davidson in February 1826. Worship services were held in various places until Wesley Chapel, the first Methodist church in Memphis, was erected. A combination church and Sunday School building, built of brick, replaced the frame building in 1845.

The present First United Methodist Church is enhanced by stained glass windows and an organ designed by Frank Roosevelt, which occupies thirty feet of wall space behind the pulpit.

Many distinguished people, including William Jennings Bryan, Senator Estes Kefauver, and many bishops, have spoken from the pulpit. In 1896, the funeral of United States Senator Isham G. Harris, who had served as Tennessee's only Confederate governor, was held here.

'alvary Episcopal, Memphis

'alvary Episcopal Church
Iemphis

'alvary was organized August 16, 1832 by Thomas Vright, a missionary to the Western District. It is elieved that the organization was accomplished in he home of Thomas Brown, Wright's long time riend. Carrying his Bible, Prayer Book, a hymnal, nd few items of clothing in his saddle bags, Wright ad ridden through West Tennessee in summer heat nd cold of winter organizing Episcopal churches all ver the district.

He arrived at the Brown's home on August 3. He tated in his "Travelogue" that he preached on the ixth of August and was taken sick and exhausted. Ie also wrote that he met friends and members of he church at "Major B's," and there Calvary Church vas organized. "Major B" may have been Thomas Brown, since Wright was a guest in his home at the ime.

This church of simple Gothic architecture, built in 1843, is the oldest church building in Memphis. It vas designed by the third rector of the church, the Reverend Phillip Alston, and built by a devout ommunicant, W. A. Bickford.

In 1881, James B. Cook, an English immigrant rchitect of Memphis, made additions and minor lterations to the building. He had previously lesigned two other fine churches in the city, Saint Mary's Catholic in 1864 and Trinity Lutheran in 1874.

Saint Mary's Catholic, Memphis

Saint Mary's Catholic Church
Memphis

This Gothic Revival building was designed by James B. Cook, a noted architect of the period. He was educated in England in the offices of Sir Charles Barry, and was a Fellow of the American Institute of Architects as well as the Royal British Institute.

Dedicated in 1870, Saint Mary's shows careful detailing and simple restraint throughout. It was located amid a largely German population, and there is a distinct twelfth century German Gothic influence here.

A tower capped with pinnacles and spire was removed in 1950 because of extensive termite damage. Removal of stucco at the same time revealed the original brick walls.

Interesting "stained glass" windows, characteristic of the late nineteenth century, incorporate paint and encaustic glass to create an unusual effect.

Much gilded ornamentation, still in good condition, adorns the inside walls, and there is handsome Gothic carving on pews, altar, and Stations of the Cross.

Beale Street Baptist, Memphis

Beale Street Baptist Church
Memphis

Before the Civil War, slaves attended church with their masters and sat in galleries built especially for them. "Scipio," a slave of Mrs. L.C. Boyd, a founder of the Second Presbyterian Church in 1844, grew tired of worshipping in galleries, the religious attitudes of White ministers, and having no freedom to express his emotions.

Having withdrawn from sitting in the White man's gallery, he began opening small places of worship of his own along Beale Street. Reverend Heck Mosby, alias "Salve," who had lost a leg some time before, was pastor of one of the storefront churches.

Out of meetings in these "preaching places," Beale Street Baptist Church was formed by Reverend Scott Keys in his home on Turley Street. Later pastors Lewis Gales and Morris Henderson moved the congregation to Beale and Fourth Streets, where they occupied the basement of a White church. This building was later destroyed by fire.

A building was procured on Main Street at Beale Street, and a White minister, Reverend Samuel G. Tillman, became pastor. In a short time a tract of land was donated to this group by the New York Baptist Society, and a church was built at Fourth and Beale Streets at a cost of $100,000.

This imposing Victorian Gothic church of brick and graystone construction, erected between 1865 and 1869, was the first brick church built by Blacks in the South. General Ulysses S. Grant delivered an address here on a visit to Memphis while he was President.

First Baptist, Memphis

First Baptist Church
Memphis

On April 3, 1839, eleven people met in the home of Spencer Hall and organized a "Missionary Baptist Church" which would later be known as First Baptist Church of Memphis. Plans for building a church were made the next day at the School House of Eugene Magenney.

In 1842, a site on Second Avenue between Adams and Washington Streets was selected for the first church building. The property, where the Shelby County courthouse now stands, was donated by Geraldus Buntyn, a prominent Memphis businessman. The church was completed in late 1846 and the first service held on January 10, 1847.

This Greek Revival church became a hospital for the Federal army, which returned it to the congregation at the end of the Civil War with definite abuse visible throughout. The yellow fever epidemic of 1879 claimed one hundred and fifty members of this church.

Major renovation took place in 1886-88, and toward the end of the nineteenth century the congregation decided to move to a new location. This time First Baptist built a handsome church at Linden and Lauderdale in 1906-07. The present building was completed at the same address in 1923.

Germantown Baptist, Memphis

ermantown Baptist Church
emphis

rganized in 1835, this congregation was originally alled New Hope Church. A church was erected on a ite donated to the congregation prior to 1851, but as burned by stragglers of the Union army in July 862. The pulpit Bible, dated 1856, was the only item aved, and it is still displayed on special occasions. he present sanctuary was built on the original site 1871.

The Germantown Baptist Church, of frame onstruction with a steeple, was in regular use until 972. The original roof has been replaced with sphalt shingles, and the old doors, twelve feet high, ave been replaced with duplications of the originals. luted pilasters at all four corners on the exterior xtend to the cornice brackets. On the north and outh sides of the building are five double hung six ver six windows.

The traditional appearance of rural churches in the nid-nineteenth century is reflected here, and this hurch is preserved as an example of religious rchitecture of the period. Weddings, christenings, nd other special events are still performed here.

mmanuel Episcopal Church
emphis

n 1874, Bishop Charles Quintard granted permission or an Episcopal service to be held in Zion Hall on eale Street. Reverend George J. Jackson, an rdained deacon, took charge of the congregation hich would become Emmanuel, and worship was eld in Zion Hall until 1883, when their first building as purchased on North Third Street between Court nd Jefferson Avenues.

Reverend Isaac Edgar Black became the first astor here and was followed by a succession of appointed pastors. In 1907, Thomas Demby became priest-in-charge, and a building site was selected at the corner of Saint Paul and Cynthia Avenues. A cruciform brick structure was completed in 1913 and was used until 1954, when it was necessary to rebuild it. The present church was dedicated in May 1956 by Bishop Theodore N. Barth.

Reverend Thomas Demby became Archdeacon and was placed in charge of the Colored Protestant Episcopal Churches in Tennessee, and later was elected Suffragan Bishop for Negro Churches in the Diocese of Arkansas and the Province of the Southwest.

The consecration of Bishop Demby on September 15, 1918, in All Saints Church, Saint Louis, brought to Emmanuel Church the distinction of being one of the few Black congregations in America to produce a bishop.

mmanuel Episcopal, Memphis

Saint Mary's Cathedral (Episcopal)
Memphis

W. Halsey Wood, an Eastern architect, died while he was designing this cathedral of late Gothic style, and L. M. Leathers of Memphis replaced him as architect. The cornerstone was laid in 1898, and the foundations and crypt were completed soon after. The congregation worshipped in this unfinished building for seven years.

In 1906 construction was resumed on the building, but it was not completed. Under the direction of

Saint Mary's Cathedral (Episcopal), Memphis

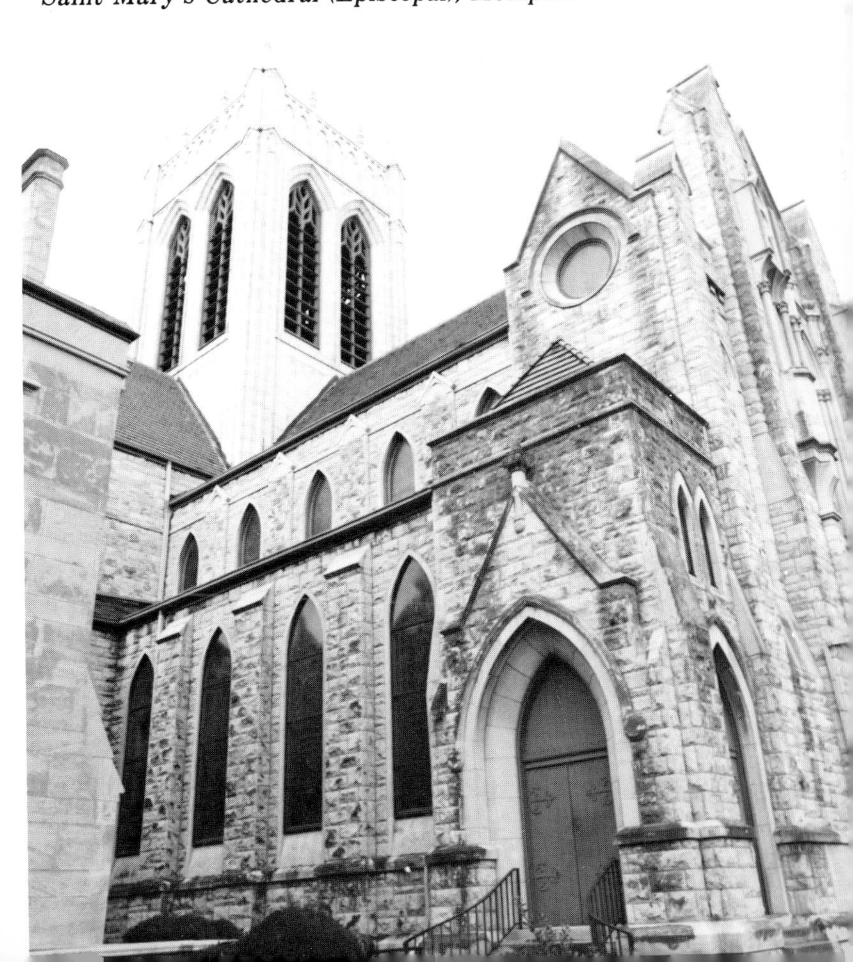

Bayard Cairns of Memphis, the cathedral was finally completed in 1925.

The interior of this cathedral has an Early English air, graced with fine craftsmanship and symbolism. Len R. Howard, of Kent, Connecticut, who studied his craft in England and America, designed, produced, and installed forty-one stained glass windows in the sanctuary. The organ has 3,173 pipes and is unique in Memphis and the Southeast.

Saint Mary's was organized by James Hervey Otey, first bishop of Tennessee, in 1856. Pews were free and open to all who wished to attend.

On January 1, 1871, Saint Mary's became a cathedral. It is the oldest Episcopal cathedral in the South, and is among the oldest in the Unied States. This was the first Episcopal church in the South to include women in the choir, the first to vest the choir, and the first to place candles and flowers on the altar.

The Victorian Gothic chapel, built in 1887 by an unknown architect, was the gift of Colonel R. B. Snowden for the use of the Sisters of Saint Mary's.

During the yellow fever epidemic of the 1870's, this cathedral remained open while few other churches did. Many people fled the city, but the priests and sisters remained in the cathedral to nurse the sick and minister to the poor. Two priests and four sisters died during the epidemic in 1878.

Meetings of labor, religious, and city government workers were held in the cathedral during the sanitation strike and other civil rights troubles of the 1960's. On the morning after the murder of Dr. Martin Luther King, a memorial service was held here. This gathering included all denominations and races, and people of all walks of life.

Morton Memorial Methodist, Monteagle

Morton Memorial Methodist Church Monteagle

Soon after 1800, a Methodist church was organized in Monteagle. The congregation shared a Union church with the Church of Christ and Cumberland Presbyterian congregations.

In 1895, plans were made for a separate building for the Methodist church. A frame building was intended, but Mrs. E. E. Hoss, wife of Bishop Hoss, influenced the congregation to use native limestone. A considerable debt resulted from this decision.

Contributions were made, much labor was done with no charge, women held ice cream suppers and a Strawberry Festival to raise money. Dr. David Morton, First General Secretary of the Board of Church Extension, secured a loan from the General Conference. Each stained glass window was given as a memorial. The cornerstone of this handsome Gothic church was unveiled in 1897.

In 1898, Dr. Morton died of blood poisoning. The congregation later changed the name to Morton Memorial. This church stands on the highest peak in the Cumberland Mountains.

Birthplace of the Cumberland Presbyterian Church Montgomery Bell State Park

On February 3, 1810, Finis Ewing, Samuel King, and Ephraim McLean met at a log cabin on Acorn Creek in Dickson County where Samuel McAdow lived in semi-retirement. The purpose of this meeting was to consider and perhaps resolve issues within the Presbytery.

They knew that resolving these issues might well result in separation of a group from the Presbyterian Church. These ministers had refused to accept the authority of the Presbytery in a political debate aimed at toning down the revivalist spirit among Tennessee churches during the "Great Awakening" which had spread throughout the state.

After a night of prayerful discussion, the decision was reached—around sunrise the next morning—to withdraw and form a new denomination, to be known as the Cumberland Presbyterian Church.

A replica of the first church building of the new denomination stands on a site inside the main entrance of Montgomery Bell State Park in Dickson County.

ear Creek Cumberland Presbyterian Church
ooresville

his church is a fine example of the vernacular othic Revival architecture found particularly in the entral highlands of Middle Tennessee. The design atures round arches, lancet windows, and taggered sawtooth brickwork.

Bear Creek Church was organized in 1814 by the everend Samuel King four years after he and three ther ministers organized the Cumberland resbyterian Church. King became the first pastor.

There is a tradition in the Orr family, whose embers were among the original church elders, hat a barn on the farm of James Porter Orr was uilt of logs from the first church building, of which o written records exist. Camp meetings were held n the church grounds from 1826 until 1833.

The second building was of brick and built about 850. Later alterations to the interior weakened the tructure to such an extent that a decision was made o raze the building and build a new one. John A. offee supervised the construction of the present hurch building, and bricks for it were made on the ite. The church was dedicated in 1898.

Regular worship was discontinued at Bear Creek hurch in 1932.

Birthplace of the Cumberland Presbyterian Church

Bear Creek Cumberland Presbyterian, Mooresville

orristown Baptist Church
orristown

orristown Baptist Church was organized out of ent Creek Baptist Church in 1803, fifty years efore the village of Morristown was organized. radition says that Reverend Isaac Barton and everend Caleb Witt were the organizing ministers.

The first building was made of logs on land onated by Benjamin Cox. That site, between herokee Drive and North Cumberland Street, is ow occupied by the Hamblen County Health epartment. The first school in Morristown was held n that log building, and the last teacher was everend William Rodgers, who in 1851 became the irst President of Mossy Creek College, now Carson-ewman College in Jefferson City.

A third church built of bricks was erected on a ew site next to the courthouse in 1870. Reacting to he new location, many members of the congregation sked, "Where will we water our horses?" The need or such basic farmland amenities was slowing the nove of Baptist churches from rural areas to towns nd villages throughout East Tennessee.

Named Morristown Baptist Church in 1858, this istoric church today provides such ministries as bus ervice, a ministry to the deaf, and radio and elevision broadcasts of both Sunday services.

Morristown Baptist

Cook's Methodist, Mount Juliet

Centenary Methodist, Morristown

Centenary Methodist Church
Morristown

When this church was first organized in 1881 by Dr. Judson S. Hill, it was called "Northern Methodist" because it was affiliated with the Northern church. Dr. Hill also founded Morristown Negro College at about the same time.

One of the oldest buildings in Hamblen County, the church dates from 1884. The original structure cost less than $3,000 to complete.

The exterior of the church is the same today as when it was originally built, and features the original stained glass windows.

Cook's Methodist Church
Mount Juliet

Soon after 1800, Reverend Fountain Pitts, a Methodist circuit rider, paused to rest under a large oak tree at the crest of a hill. While contemplating his further journey and the purpose of his mission for his church, he dreamed of a house of worship on the site where he and his horse had spent the past hours. He prayed for that dream to be fulfilled.

In 1819, the Cook family donated land on that hill and Cook's Camp Ground was organized. A brush arbor was built as the first place of worship in that community.

In January 1848, Less M. Cook gave land on which to build a church. It is believed that the first building was of frame construction.

The present white frame church of vernacular Gothic construction was built in 1898. Major renovation was accomplished in 1955.

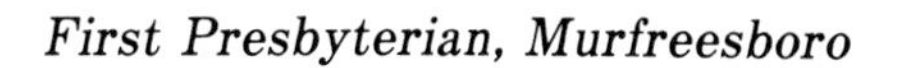

First Presbyterian, Murfreesboro

First Presbyterian, Murfreesboro

First Presbyterian Church
Murfreesboro

A school house on a hill near Murfree Springs was the first meeting place for the small group of Presbyterians which later founded the First Presbyterian Church of Murfreesboro. Later they met in another school house located between Academy and Maney Streets.

The first church building stood on East Vine Street where the city cemetery is now located. Inside, the building contained galleries for organ, choir, and slaves.

When the Rutherford County courthouse burned in 1822 while Murfreesboro was the capital of Tennessee, the General Assembly met in the Presbyterian Church. James K. Polk, Clerk of the Senate, Sam Houston, Adjutant General, and Andrew Jackson attended many sessions of the Assembly.

Union forces occupied Murfreesboro early in the Civil War, seized the Presbyterian Church, demolished it, and used the bricks to construct ovens at their camping grounds. The church bell, hidden by some women of the church, was the only thing saved.

At the close of the war, Dr. William Eaglestons, pastor from 1829 to 1866, led in constructing a new sanctuary at the corner of East College and North Spring Streets in 1888. This building was destroyed by a tornado in 1913; the present building of Greek Revival design, completed in 1914, stands on the same site.

Among the distinguished members of First Presbyterian Church was General Joseph Dickson, who saw military service in North Carolina and was a member of the United States House of Representatives.

First Baptist, Murfreesboro

First Baptist Church
Murfreesboro

There were Baptist Churches in Rutherford County as early as 1800, but First Baptist was not organized until 1843. After meeting for a time in the homes of James Franklin Fletcher and Thomas Maney, sixteen persons met in Fletcher's School House and organized the church on June 9, 1843. The first church building was completed at Spring and Sevier Streets in early 1849.

In 1861, the Confederate army occupied Murfreesboro and raised the Confederate flag above the courthouse. Dr. James Madison Pendleton, pastor of First Baptist Church, was an ardent supporter of the Union, and it was reported that he kept a supply of food beside an unlatched door of his home in case he and his wife should need to escape town at a moment's notice. Feeling unsafe, they did leave Murfreesboro in 1862, each going away alone.

The building was used by both Union and Confederate armies and left in a deplorable condition. Plans were made in 1868 for a new church which was completed in 1870.

The present church was completed in 1920 one block from the Rutherford County courthouse.

East Main Street Church of Christ, Murfreesboro

East Main Street Church of Christ
Murfreesboro

This red brick building, erected in 1859, is one of the oldest in downtown Murfreesboro and features unique stained glass windows. It was rebuilt in 1901.

Brigadier General James A. Garfield, later President of the United States, conducted worship services here during the Civil War. Among the treasures of this congregation is a sterling silver communion service given by Garfield.

The church was organized in the Rutherford County courthouse in 1833. The congregation worshipped in its own building on Vine Street near Lytle's Creek until 1859, when the present site was purchased at East Main and Academy Streets.

There are no minutes of this congregation before the Civil War, but it is known that David Lipscomb preached here on many occasions.

First United Methodist, Murfreesboro

First United Methodist Church
Murfreesboro

As a result of revival meetings at Windrow's Camp Ground, a Methodist church was organized in Murfreesboro in 1820. The forty members worshipped in a home on College Street until a small building was erected on land donated by John Lytle on Maple Street.

Records show 128 members in 1828, with one third of them being Black. Murfreesboro became a station in 1830, and Reverend Robert Paine became the first pastor.

The Tennessee Methodist Conference met here in 1828. Cullen T. Carter, writing in the History of the Tennessee Conference, stated that a delegation of Cherokee Indians, headed by Reverend Turtle Fields, attended the conference on December 4, 1828.

A new building was erected in 1843 on Church Street opposite the present church site. It was used for more than forty years but was severely damaged during the Civil War, and was eventually replaced with another building. The cornerstone of the present Gothic church was laid on March 20, 1955.

Two former pastors of this church, Robert Paine and Paul B. Kern, became bishops.

Central Christian Church
Murfreesboro

Alexander Campbell preached in the Methodist Church in Murfreesboro in 1833, and shortly thereafter a dozen believers organized the Murfreesboro Christian Church. Property was purchased near Lytle Creek, but the congregation grew and a new building was erected in 1858 at East Main and Academy Streets.

A division occurred within the Christian/Church of Christ movement toward the end of the nineteenth century over the issues of missions and the use of instrumental music in services, and in 1906 the more fundamentalist Church of Christ faction separated from the Christian Church.

In Murfreesboro, the Church of Christ followers were in the majority, and in August 1908 sixty-one members withdrew and formed Central Christian Church. The remainder of the congregation constituted the East Main Street Church of Christ.

In 1909, the state convention of Christian Churches met in Murfreesboro, and enough money was raised to build a church, which was completed in 1912; this Neoclassical structure is still in use.

Central Christian, Murfreesboro

First Presbyterian Church
Downtown Presbyterian Church
Nashville

Presbyterianism first came to Nashville with Reverend Thomas Craighead in 1785. He became president of Davidson Academy, the ancestor of Cumberland College, the University of Nashville, and Peabody College, and preached on Sundays in the academy building on Gallatin Road. Another Presbyterian minister and scholar, William Hume, came to Nashville in 1801 and "preached wherever I could find someone to listen." He was later principal of the Nashville Female Academy.

First Presbyterian Church was itself founded in 1814 by the Reverend Gideon Blackburn and seven loyal members. Their first building was erected at Fifth and Church in 1816. This church burned January 29, 1832, and was replaced by a large Greek Revival building with a 150-foot tall spire, which burned in 1848.

Among the prominent members here were John Bell and Felix Grundy; both Sam Houston and Andrew Jackson attended services. James K. Polk was inaugurated as governor here in 1839. Mrs. Polk was a member for many years; her pew is still labeled. Pews were auctioned to the highest bidder in 1833, but an annual rent had to be maintained; the practice was discontinued in 1944.

Mrs. Felix Grundy organized the first Sunday School in Tennessee in a small building near the church. Since Bible teaching had been excluded from public schools in 1819, Mrs. Grundy sought to give instruction to children in the area. Fifteen children enrolled in her first class to study the New Testament and Webster's Spelling Book.

In 1833, John Todd Edgar became pastor; he served until 1860 and achieved such prominence that a city-wide day of mourning was declared at his death. Referred to by Henry Clay as the greatest orator in America, he conducted the funeral of Andrew Jackson at the Hermitage in 1845.

On Easter Sunday, 1851, the congregation's third building was dedicated. This handsome building was designed by noted architect William Strickland, who designed the Tennessee State Capitol, Saint Mary's Catholic Church, and many other notable buildings in the eastern United States.

Downtown Presbyterian, Nashville

First Presbyterian, Nashville

During the early part of the nineteenth century, there was a sudden interest in things Egyptian, beginning with Napoleon's invasion of Egypt and spurred by reports of archaeological discoveries in the 1830's and 40's. Although the "Egyptian Revival" style of architecture was not uncommon during the period, little of it remains today; this church is considered the best preserved example in the United States.

The choice of the Egyptian motif has often been questioned, but, as the logical Presbyterians have long pointed out, why is Egyptian architecture more pagan or objectionable than that of Classical Greece? The congregation extended the Egyptian theme when, beginning in 1880, the two front columns were added and the interior remodeled.

The interior pilasters and the moldings and pediments around the windows were part of Strickland's original design, but the perspective paintings of receding columns were added when the amen corners beside the pulpit were closed off. In 1887 stained glass windows, also featuring Egyptian motifs, were installed. The walnut pulpit was built in 1895.

During the Civil War the building was used as the principle Union hospital in the city, and worship was discontinued for several years. By contrast, during World War II, the church opened a lounge for servicemen and provided free food and lodging on weekends.

In 1955, Doctor Walter Rowe Courtenay led the First Presbyterian congregation to a new location on Franklin Road in Oak Hill. A group of members who wanted to remain downtown was able to buy the old church and reorganize as Downtown Presbyterian. Although most of the furnishings were taken to Oak Hill, a four thousand pound bell given by Adelicia Acklen still hangs at the downtown church. From 1874 to 1897 it served as the city fire alarm.

The complex of buildings at First Presbyterian in Oak Hill, designed by architect Francis B. Warfield to blend with the house already located there, includes an imposing Georgian sanctuary with a tall steeple. On October 27, 1974, a pipe organ built by Rudolf von Beckerath was dedicated. Oak Hill School, located on the church property, is celebrating its twenty-fifth anniversary in 1986. The private elementary school provides classes for pre-school through sixth grade.

Today both First Presbyterian and Downtown Presbyterian have several ministries in common. In 1986 they held a Homecoming reunion with services at Fifth and Church and a dinner and celebration at Oak Hill. They are further joined under the pastorate of Doctor William Turner Bryant, senior minister of both.

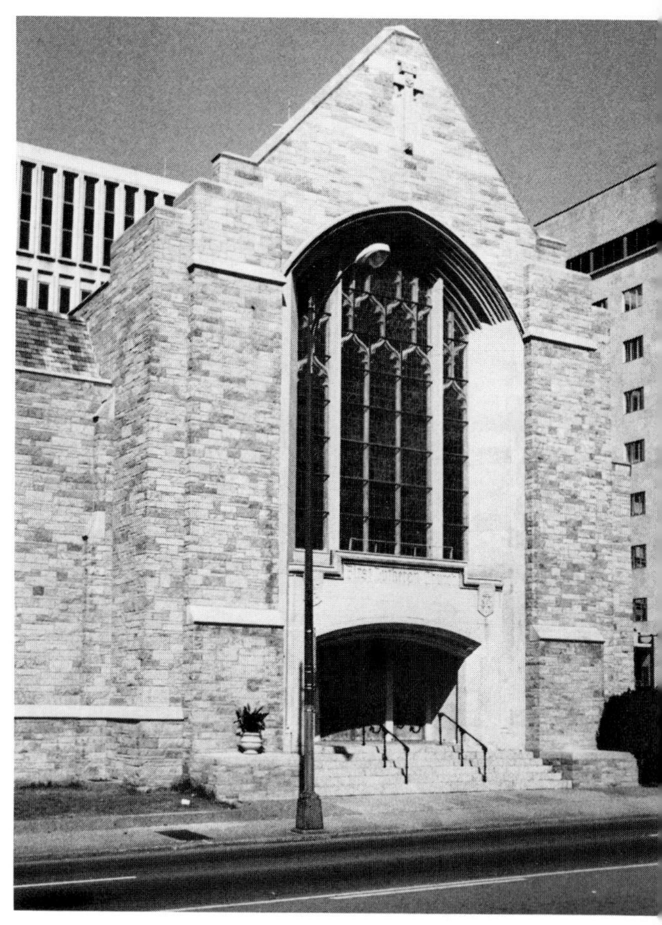

First Lutheran, Nashville

First Lutheran Church Nashville

While attending a meeting of the General Synod of the Lutheran Church in 1859, Reverend William Jenkins, pastor of a Lutheran congregation in Shelbyville, persuaded Reverend Herman Eggers to go to Nashville and work among Lutherans there.

Reverend Eggers organized First Lutheran Church in Nashville on the last Sunday in August. He had preached his first sermon to a group of German-speaking settlers in the Davidson County Courthouse one month before. Worship was held in the German Methodist Church during the Civil War.

In 1867, a house of worship was built on North Market Street, now Second Avenue North, near the Public Square. Worship was conducted there in the German language only until 1878, when Reverend F. E. Perschau preached in English for the first time. German language services continued until after 1900.

The First Lutheran congregation purchased the First Baptist Church building on North Summer Street. Adolphus Heiman, a noted architect from Germany, had designed that Gothic building. Lindsley Hall, which later housed the Children's

Museum, Belmont Mansion, and his home on Jefferson Street were designed by Heiman.

It was during the pastorate of Reverend I. W. Gernert, who served the church for thiry-six years, that the present Gothic church was dedicated in 1951. It was constructed of Briar Hill stone with white Indiana limestone trim, and was designed by Marr and Holman, architects.

The sanctuary features twelve stained glass windows, six of which had graced the church on Summer Street. The memorial chapel is dedicated to Henry and Tony Sudekum, and there is a special Children's Chapel which contains windows from the old church on Summer Street. The altar is of Tennessee marble. A Schantz organ was installed in 1963.

Saint Patrick's Catholic, Nashville

Saint Patrick's Catholic Church Nashville

Saint Patrick's Church, built in the Second Empire Style, is relatively unchanged from its original appearance and condition. Built in 1892, it served an Irish Catholic community and six itinerant families of house painters and horse traders who returned to Nashville in May of each year to bury their dead. On occasion, a few still return to bury the dead in Calvary Cemetery after funeral services in Saint Patrick's Church.

Saint Patrick's has long been in the forefront of service to the poor and destitute in the community, and has helped coordinate the efforts of other Nashville churches.

First Church of Christ, Scientist Nashville

The First Church of Christ, Scientist, was founded in 1902 by local students of Mary Baker Eddy, founder of the movement in Boston, Massachusetts in 1879.

The cornerstone for the building was laid in 1961, and it was completed and dedicated a year later. Designed by John E. Sutter, Nashville architect, this red brick church of Colonial design features four Greek columns and a seventy-seven foot high steeple.

At the rear of the church stands a renovated farm house built before 1830 and now used for Sunday School. The church received an award for "outstanding efforts toward the preservation of Davidson County's architectural heritage" from the Nashville Historical Commision for the restoration of this building.

In 1954, First Church of Christ, Scientist and Second Church of Christ, Scientist, which was organized in 1921, united into one church. A Christian Science Reading Room, at 202 Sixth Avenue, North, has been maintained since 1902.

First Church of Christ, Scientist, Nashville

First Unitarian-Universalist, Nashville

First Unitarian-Universalist Church Nashville

A Unitarian congregation existed in Nashville from the mid-1840's, but the unpopularity of the church's anti-slavery position led to the group's disbanding in 1853.

A second church was formed in 1916 and disbanded in 1934 because of the Depression. Gean Morgan, a member of both the 1916 and the present church, was honored with the denomination's "Unsung U-U Award" in 1975.

Born out of an informal fellowship on the Vanderbilt University campus in 1946, the First Unitarian-Universalist Church of Nashville was founded on May 12, 1950. It fulfilled requirements for church status in 1954 and is an affiliate of the Thomas Jefferson District of the Unitarian-Universalist Association.

The congregation met in a brick house for several years before building a stone church on Woodmont Boulevard in 1962. The first service in the new church was held on Christmas Eve of that year, with plastic covering the unglazed windows. This building, reminiscent of Frank Lloyd Wright's designs, is the work of Bruce Draper, Nashville architect.

The church was active in the Civil Rights movement of the 1960's and for years was home to a cooperative nursery. It now maintains a school and participates in a wide range of social, educational, and civic activities.

First Church of the Nazarene Nashville

James Octavius McClurkan, father of the Wesleyan movement in Middle Tennessee, arrived in Nashville in 1897. Here he met John Thomas Benson, Sr., a partner in a brokerage firm of Cummins, Benson, and McKay. Together they became prominent in the founding of the Nazarene church.

In 1898, a church building constructed by Tulip Street Methodist Church during the Civil War on Fifth Street between Fatherland and Russel Streets was secured for use by the Nazarene Church. The owner of the building, James H. Moore, charged no rent for the building.

In 1900, the Hynes School Building at Fifth and Jo Johnston Streets was bought for five thousand dollars. That same year three thousand dollars was raised for foreign missions, and W. A. Farmer went to China as a missionary.

In 1901, Bible Training School was opened with W. M. Tidwell as the first student. The Training School later became Trevecca Nazarene College. No tuition was charged, and room and board was ten dollars per month.

In 1916, Woodland Street Presbyterian Church at 510 Woodland Street was severely damaged by fire. The fire-damaged building was bought and restored by the Nazarene congregation, which moved there in 1917.

The present Greek Revival style red brick church, built at that same location, seats one thousand people.

First Church of the Nazarene, Nashville

First Baptist, Nashville

First Baptist Church
Nashville

The Baptist Church in Davidson County can be traced back to 1794, when one church was organized north of Nashville; another was built on Mill Creek on the south side of Nashville in 1797. James Whitsett, leader of the Mill Creek Church, held a series of revival meetings in 1820 which led to the founding of First Baptist Church.

The new First Baptist congregation met for worship where Hume-Fogg High School now stands in a building previously used by the Methodist Church. They soon built the largest and most impressive church in the city on Church Street between Sixth and Seventh Avenues. The inauguration of Sam Houston as Governor of Tennessee whas held in the new Baptist Church in 1827.

When Alexander Campbell arrived in Nashville preaching in a number of churches, many members of First Baptist Church discarded their beliefs in favor of the "Current Reformation" taught by Campbell. In 1830, five members remained in the Baptist Church but returned to Mill Creek Church. The remaining members left the Baptist faith and formed the Vine Street Christian Church.

Beginning in 1835, First Baptist Church was reorganized under the leadership of R.B.C. Howell, who served the church until 1850 and again from 1857 to 1867. From 1851 to 1857 he was president of the Southern Baptist Convention.

Among Howell's accomplishments was the founding of *The Baptist*, a periodical with a nationwide readership. In 1848 J. R. Graves became editor of *The Baptist* and led an "exclusivist" movement, advocating withdrawal of fellowship from other denominations, since Baptist churches were the only true churches. He bitterly attacked Howell, who urged a more moderate position, and was tried and excluded from the church in 1858. He remained editor of *The Baptist*, however, and the controversy persisted.

A new Gothic church was erected on Summer Street (Fifth Avenue North) between Deaderick and Union Streets. Completed in 1841, this building was used until 1884, when it was sold to the First Lutheran congregation. For a year while the new church was under construction, the First Baptist congregation worshipped in the Vine Street Temple. The third building was dedicated March 14, 1886.

First Baptist Church has enjoyed a close relationship with the Baptist Sunday School Board, established in 1891 under the leadership of Dr. J. M. Frost. At one point the First Baptist Sunday School became the testing ground for Board materials, and registration and attendance more than doubled. In 1924, the first radio station in Nashville, WCBQ, was started at First Baptist.

The present church was completed in 1970. Its design is cruciform, with the distinct impression of an Early Christian Basilica. The handsome tower which graced the previous building remains. This blending of architectural forms has created an unusual building of beauty and charm.

Strother's Meeting House, Nashville

Strother's Meeting House
Nashville

The first annual conference of the Methodist Church in Middle Tennessee met on October 2, 1802, in Strother's Meeting House in Sumner County with Bishop Francis Asbury presiding.

This small log building has been called "the Traveling Church." Later in its history, the church was dismantled and the logs moved to Red River Pike, and again dismantled and moved to a large barn. The building in which the first conference of the Methodist Church met was used as a corn crib for seventy years. It has beeen moved again and now has an honored place on the Scarritt College campus.

Among the artifacts on display there are eye glasses belonging to Mrs. Elizabeth Combs, who lent them to Bishop Asbury when he left his at home; a mourner's bench hand-hewn from timber cut in the area; shop-forged nails; a leather-bound trunk which belonged to Bishop McKendree; Bishop Asbury's chair; a bust of John Wesley made in 1790; and saddle bags used by early circuit riding preachers.

Strother's Meeting House, interior

Saddle bags of early circuit riding preachers

Granny White Church of Christ
Nashville

In 1903 College Church was organized near the David Lipscomb College campus, and worhip was held in a building on the campus for forty-one years. Although it was concerned with religious life of the college students, the church has always numbered citizens having no connection with the college in its membership.

The present brick and stone church of Romanesque Gothic architecture was constructed in 1954. Missionaries to Africa, British Columbia, and Ontario have gone from this church.

Lindsley Avenue Church of Christ
Nashville

Lindsley Avenue Church was formed in a religious service led by David Lipscomb and attended by three women and a little boy in 1855. The new congregation constructed a building in 1894, and in 1920 they purchased the building which they now occupy from a Methodist church.

This unusual Gothic church with a round tower and turret features many interesting stained glass windows.

Granny White Church of Christ, Nashville

Lindsley Avenue Church of Christ, Nashville

Temple Ohabai Sholom, Nashville

Saint Ann's Episcopal, Nashville

Saint Ann's Episcopal Church Nashville

Called Saint Stephen's when it was organized in 1858, this congregation worshipped in a school building on Fatherland Street until their first church was completed in 1860. That simple but distinctive Gothic building stood on Boscobel and Fourth Streets on land donated by Dr. John Shelby, who owned a large tract of land in the area. The name was later changed to Saint Ann's in honor of a cousin of Dr. Shelby.

The present red brick church of Gothic design with white stone ornamentation features a Tiffany window in the front door. Numerous Victorian stained glass windows in this church constitute one of the finest collections in the southeastern part of the United States.

During the fire which swept over a wide area of East Nashville, Saint Ann's was saved by the day-long vigilance of the faithful sexton, Julien Campbell. Records state that he climbed to the roof, where he fought the oncoming blaze with brooms and buckets of water. Campbell served as sexton here for many years.

he Temple, Congregation Ohabai Sholom
ashville

 permanent Jewish community had developed in
ashville in the late 1840's, when a group began
eeting in the home of Isaac Garritson. In July 1851
 benevolent society was founded and the land for a
emetery purchased. The first Jewish congregation
n Tennessee, chartered on March 2, 1854, took the
ame Kahl Kodesh Mogen David in honor of
avidson County.

Alexander Iser of New York arrived in Nashville
or High Holy Days in the fall of 1852 and later
ecame Nashville's first rabbi. He served five years
efore leaving the post to enter the business world
ere. He was followed by Emanuel Marcusson, who
emained two years; during that time, the
ongregation rented a building on North Market
treet and remodeled it for a synagogue.

In 1859, a group which included Iser split from the
ogen David and formed Kahl Kodesh Ohava Emes.
he two congregations were reunited in 1867 and
ook the name Ohavai Sholom; the spelling was
hanged to Ohabai in 1955.

A Reform congregation called B'nai Yeshurun was
ounded in 1864 and lasted into the mid-1870's. At
hat time, Ohavai Sholom joined the Union of
merican Hebrew Congregations, and the smaller
eform group eventually disbanded.

Three rabbis have served this congregation for
ore than twenty years each—Isidore Lewinthal,
ulius Mark, and Randall Falk. All were respected
eaders in both Jewish and Christian communities
nd did much to elevate the status of Nashville
ewry.

In 1874, the cornerstone of Vine Street Temple
as laid with Rabbi Isaac M. Wise and ex-President
ndrew Johnson present. Dedication was held in
876 following completion of this striking Byzantine
uilding on the east side of Seventh Avenue North.

In 1955 the congregation moved to its present
oncrete and stone structure on Harding Road.

cKendree United Methodist Church
ashville

cKendree, located on Church Street, is often
eferred to as "The Mother of Methodism in
ennessee." Its history can be traced to 1787, when
reachers and laymen arrived in the middle district.
 stone building just twenty feet square and with a
irt floor and unglazed windows, built on the Public
quare in 1790, was the first place of worship for
ethodists in Nashville. One thousand people heard
ishop Asbury preach here in 1800. James
obertson, founder of Nashville, was a steward of
his church.

McKendree Methodist, Nashville

After six or seven years, this building was removed to make room for the courthouse. The congregation met in members' homes and in the public jail until 1812, when they moved into a larger building on Broadway where Hume-Fogg High School now stands. The largest church in Nashville, this building was used by the state legislature from 1813 to 1817.

In 1818, a new building was erected at Third Avenue and Church Street. Called Spring Street Church, it covered the entire block between Third and Fourth Avenues. In 1819, the minister's wife reported that Nashville was a town of two distilleries and three churches.

The establishment of Sunday Schools in Nashville by the Presbyterians met with some opposition from the Methodist congregation. The church in 1820 bore a sign stating: "No desecration of the Holy Sabbath by teaching on the Sabbath in this church." Methodist Sunday Schools were established in 1822, however, by Reverend Thomas Maddin.

In 1833, this growing church moved once again. That building at 523 Church Street, where McKendree Church now stands, then contained the largest sanctuary in the South and the second largest in the United States.

Bishop William McKendree delivered the dedication sermon on October 15, 1833. He gave his last sermon here November 15, 1834, seated in a chair, since he was by that time too feeble to stand. He died in 1835 and is buried on the Vanderbilt University campus.

The 1833 building was replaced by a handsome church featuring three tall spires, dedicated by Bishop Holland N. McTyeire January 29, 1879. It burned the same year, but was insured; the congregation met at the Vine Street Temple until a new building of the same basic design was built in 1882.

The middle spire blew off in 1897; in 1905 construction was begun to replace the spire, install stained glass, and do other repairs. On July 4, a workman left the rear window open and apparently a stray firecracker ignited the building, which burned down.

The cornerstone of the present Greek Revival church was laid on November 9, 1907. The dedication was held on October 12, 1912.

It was at McKendree that the first Women's Missionary Society of the Methodist Church in the South was organized. It was in the sanctuary of McKendree Church that the funeral of President James K. Polk was conducted on June 16, 1849; several Tennessee governors, including Andrew Johnson, were inaugurated; and six Methodist Bishops were consecrated.

Congregation Sherith Israel
Nashville

Records do not reveal the exact reasons for the divisions in the Jewish community in Nashville in the late nineteenth century, but it seems clear that the drift of Congregation Ohavai Sholom into the Reform movement led to efforts to keep Orthodox Judaism alive.

In 1871 and again in 1887, a group called the "Ungarischer Unterstetzung Verein of Nashville or the Hungarian Benevolent Society" received charters from the state. This society both maintained a cemetery and conducted religious services for the Orthodox community. It later merged with fraternal societies known as the Independent Order of Brith Abraham and the Knights of Joseph.

In 1905 a group from the Hungarian Society organized a congregation known as Sherith Israel (Remnants of Israel) and purchased a house on Fifth Avenue North. In 1920 a synagogue was built on this property.

In 1945 property was bought for a Hebrew School on West End a few blocks away from Adath Israel's building. On May 2, 1948, a "cavalcade of cars" brought the Torahs to the site of the present synagogue. This building was completed in the early 1960's.

Among the dedicated leaders of this congregation was Herman Saltzman, Rabbi from the 1890's until 1928, who never accepted pay for his services and therefore felt entitled, he said, to say whatever he liked. Reverend Aaron Abramson served the congregation as cantor, *schocket*, and *mohel* for fifty years. Zalman I. Posner, the present rabbi, has served for a total of thirty-six years and maintained and encouraged the Akiva School for twenty-eight.

Congregation Sherith Israel, Nashville

West End Synagogue, Nashville

West End Synagogue, Congregation Adath Israel Nashville

This Conservative congregation, also known as Adas Israel and Adath Yisroel, grew out of the Vine Street congregation when the latter began to embrace Reform customs. A charter was received in 1876 and cemetery property purchased; daily services were held in the homes of members and services for High Holy Days in rented halls until 1886, when a house on North Market Street was bought and remodeled.

In 1897 the first full-time rabbi was appointed, and on September 13, 1902, a new synagogue was dedicated on Gay Street between Vine and High Streets. The congregation then had 150 members, and had eliminated the separate seating of men and women—one of the causes that had led them to separate from Ohavai Sholom.

When the Gay Street Synagogue was reclaimed with the entire area under the Capitol Redevelopment Plan, the congregation purchased and remodeled a house on West End, moving there in 1947. In 1950 a new, modern sanctuary was completed, to which a chapel and schoolrooms were added during the 1960's.

Church of the Assumption of the Blessed Virgin Mary Nashville

Few churches in the United States can match the Church of the Assumption in its gift to the clergy, having produced an archbishop and a cardinal. It was here that John A. Floersh, Archbishop of Louisville, and Samuel Cardinal Stritch, the first American appointed to the Roman Curia, were baptized. During its first one hundred years, Precious Blood Fathers, Franciscan Fathers, a Benedictine Priest, and a Dominican Priest ministered to this congregation.

This second oldest Catholic Church began as a parish church under the supervision of Richard Pius Miles, first Bishop of Nashville. Many German families had settled in the area, so Miles brought to Nashville a Flemish priest who was fluent in German, Reverend Ivo Schacht. It was Reverend Schacht who acquired the land for a house of worship.

The land was donated by Dr. David T. McGavock, whose father owned twenty-five thousand acres on both sides of the Cumberland River. The deed stated that a portion of the land was to be used for "a neat Roman Catholic church or chapel, to be used forever as such church or chapel." Bricks in the north wall of the church are from the Holy Rosary Church on Campbell's Hill, the first Catholic church in

Nashville. The dedication ceremony took place on August 14, 1859.

The Union army commandeered this church in December 1864. Much vandalism and plundering resulted. Among the debris was found a small silver plate bearing the inscription "Presented to the German Catholic Church by G. H. and J. F. Wessell and A. Roth, 1860." The plate had been attached to a chalice given to Assumption Church by these men; it is now attached to another chalice and is in use today.

Church of the Assumption, Nashville

Cathedral of the Incarnation, Nashville

Cathedral of the Incarnation
Nashville

The Cathedral of the Incarnation, of Romanesque architecture, is the third cathedral of the Diocese of Nashville. The first was erected by Bishop Miles on Campbell's Hill, now Capitol Hill; the second was the present Saint Mary's Church at 328 Fifth Avenue North.

Land was purchased by Bishop Thomas Sebastian Byrne on West End Avenue, and the cathedral was built in 1914. It was reported that "people thought he was insane to purchase land so far out in the country for a cathedral. Time has proved him to be foresighted."

Fred Asmus, Sr., is credited as the architect of the Cathedral, and Bishop Byrne and a group of architects in Rome collaborated to model the building after Saint Martin's on the Hill, which still stands in Rome. The tower, rising one hundred feet, was copied from Saint Damose, another Roman church. The Cathedral resembles a typical Roman basilica.

The sanctuary is decorated in thirteenth century Renaissance style and features the colors old rose, blue, and gold. The main altar and both side altars are of Carrera marble imported from Italy, and the wainscoting on the lower portion of the walls is lined with marble. The roof, twenty-two supporting columns, and twenty-six pilasters are made of scalioli, a special blend of sculptured mortar. The ceiling, the first of its kind in the United States, is imbedded with gold. The chandelier is of solid brass.

The baptistry is a replica of the baptismal font designed by Michelangelo in Saint Peter's Basilica in Rome. It is one-eighth the size of the one in Italy.

The Cathedral was dedicated on July 26, 1914, and Nashville newspapers described it as "one of the most churchly, ornate, and magnificent edifices south of the Ohio River." The fourteen stations of the cross, having the appearance of ivory, were presented by members or families of the parish.

Cathedral of the Incarnation (interior)

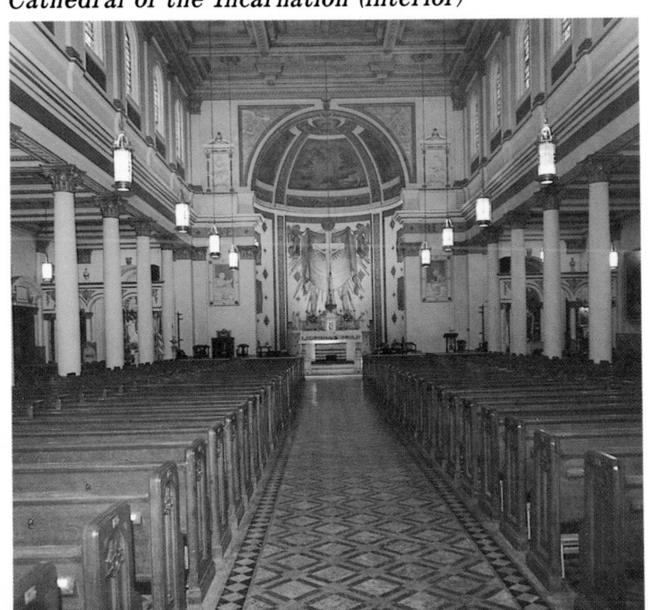

West End United Methodist (interior)

West End United Methodist, Nashville

West End United Methodist Church
Nashville

In 1868, members of McKendree Methodist Church organized a Sunday School near the corner of Church Street and Fifteenth Avenue, with John H. Baskett as superintendent. This building was in a bad state of repair, and the school closed during the winter months.

In the spring of 1869, West Nashville Mission was organized with eight members in a building known as "the old barracks" near the site of the old school. In 1873, the mission became a station with a full-time pastor and took the name West End Church.

A building site was purchased at the corner of West End Avenue and Sixteenth Street and a simple wooden building was erected. The church was dedicated on January 9, 1875, by D. C. Kelly. Children and teachers of the Sunday School collected thirty-five dollars to help pay for a small organ.

West End Church worshipped with a neighbor church, Moore Memorial Presbyterian (now Westminster Presbyterian) while a new sanctuary was built. The old building was later moved to a site near the Vanderbilt Stadium, where it was the place of worship for Blakemore Methodist Church for many years.

West End Methodist has long had a close relationship with Vanderbilt University, a Methodist institution founded with funds donated by Commodore Vanderbilt. West End Church and the chapel at Vanderbilt were originally listed together by the Conference.

By 1899, West End was furnishing many leaders for the Annual Conference. In that year, D. C. Scales became president of the Methodist Sunday School Board, Dr. W. F. Tillett was president of the Board of Trustees of Martin College and of the Conference Board of Trustees, Chancellor J. H. Kirkland was a member of the Conference General Board of Education, and Dr. W. R. Lambuth and Dr. W. F. Tillett were elected delegates to the General Conference.

In 1923, the West End Board of Trustees made application for a loan, "to aid in building a church to meet the needs of the University." The present West End site was purchased the next year and a building committee consisting of Andrew B. Benedict, John W. Barton, Cornelius A. Craig, Allen H. Meadors and Harry P. Murrey was named. A Religious Education Building was completed in October 1929, but dreams of a new sanctuary were dimmed by the Great Depression of the 1930's. The congregation numbered more than two thousand at this time.

In late 1929, West End Congregation moved to Neely Chapel on the Vanderbilt campus for what they expected to be a temporary arrangement. They worshipped there for more than ten years. The present Gothic church, built of Tennessee sandstone, was dedicated on April 11, 1948.

Christ Church, Episcopal Nashville

James Hervey Otey arrived in Middle Tennessee in 1825 and organized St. Paul's Episcopal Church in Franklin in 1828. Soon he began riding a borrowed horse to Nashville on Sunday afternoons, where he held worship services in the Masonic Hall. It was from this ministry that Christ Church was organized in 1829. Beginning with Otey, nine rectors of Christ Church have become bishops.

The first congregation included a young lawyer from New England, Francis B. Fogg, and his accomplished wife, Mary Middleton Rutledge, both of whose grandfathers had signed the Declaration of Independence. Among the first vestrymen were Fogg, John Shelby, who owned a large estate across the Cumberland River, and Thomas Claiborne, who became the first senior warden of the church as well as first Grand Master of the Masonic Order in Tennessee. Later, Captain William Driver, the sea captain who named the American flag "Old Glory," was added to the list of vestrymen.

Mrs. Fogg became a leader of women in Christ Church in raising money to feed the poor of the neighborhood and to buy a lot on Church Street on which the first building was constructed.

On July 5, 1830, the cornerstone was laid for a new church at the corner of Spring and High Streets, later the site of Harvey's Department Store at Sixth and Church.

On July 9, 1831, pews in the church were auctioned at prices ranging from $60 to $182 each. This action was taken at least in part to raise money, but only owners of pews could vote in parish meetings. The discontent and dissention caused by ownership of pews plagued the church for more than eighty years, until it was abolished in 1918.

Work began on the present building, a fine example of Victorian Gothic architecture, in 1891, and the congregation met in the Jewish Temple until it was completed. Located on Broadway at Ninth Avenue North, it was the work of Francis H. Kimball, who was trained under William Burges, a noted English Gothicist.

The church is constructed of Sewanee limestone, a gift of the University of the South. Bowling Green stone was used for the trim and the tower, which was not completed until 1947.

The interior was created under the direction of Silas McBee and contains some of the most unusual and spectacular stained glass windows in the South. The altar is reputed to be the finest work of Melchior Thoni, a noted Swiss immigrant woodcarver. Each of the capitals of the granite columns is different, as in early Christian churches built with materials from ruined pagan temples.

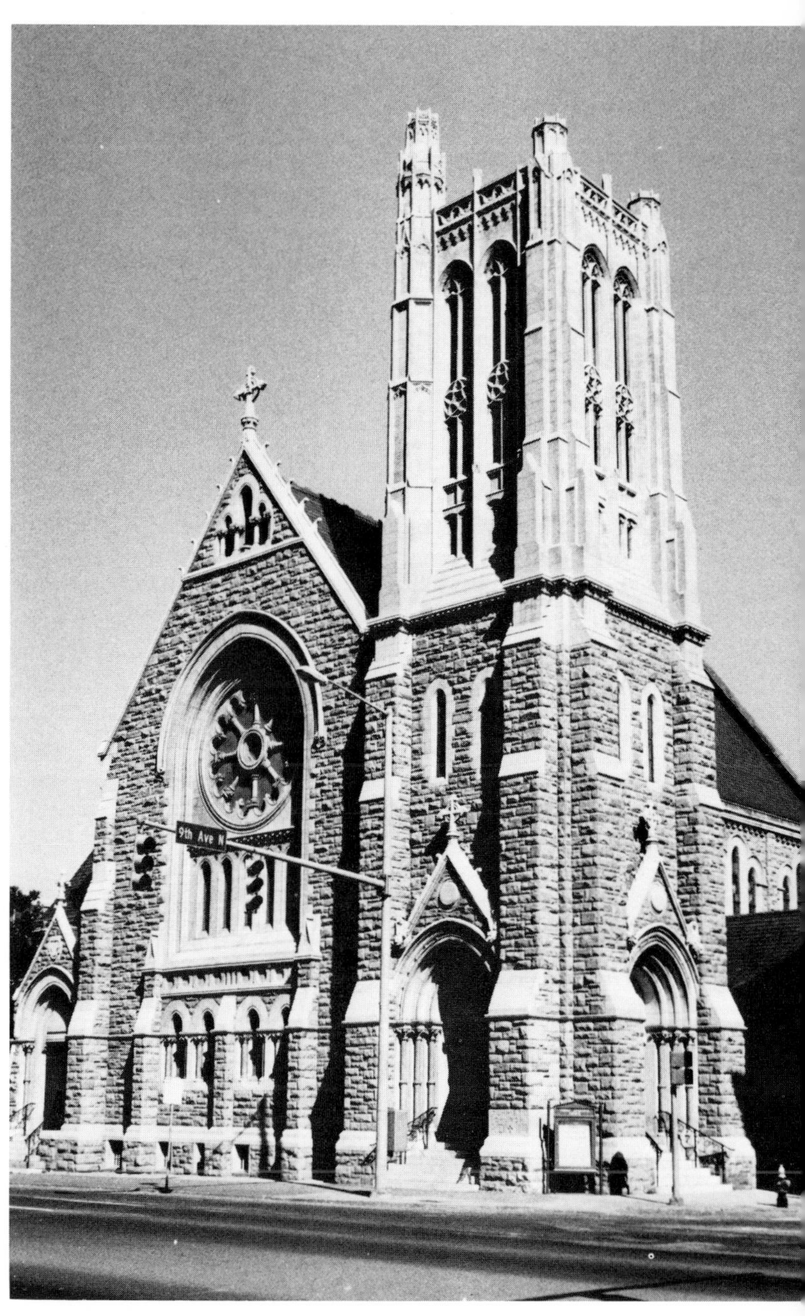

Christ Church Episcopal, Nashville

Christ Church Episcopal (interior at Christmas)

Tulip Street Methodist (detail)

Tulip Street Methodist

(interior at Christmas)

Tulip Street Methodist, Nashville

Holy Trinity Episcopal Church
Nashville

Holy Trinity Church is a fine example of Old World Gothic Revival architecture. This church, built of blue limestone, was especially designed for the small triangular lot on which it has stood since 1853.

The Reverend Charles Tomes, third rector of Christ Church Episcopal who married Henrietta Otey, daughter of Bishop James Hervey Otey, conceived the idea of a church in South Nashville as early as 1849. Along with Reverend John Philip Ingraham, a missionary sent to Christ Church Parish from the Wisconsin Board of Missions, he opened Saint Paul's Mission on Sumner Street (modern Fifth Avenue) on September 23, 1849. Soon the mission was elevated to a parish and plans were made to build a church to be called The Church of the Holy Trinity.

Mr. N. W. Wetmore, a real estate dealer in Edgefield, gave a lot for the building and plans were drawn by Frank Mills and Henry Dudley from New York. These men favored the Gothic Revival architecture which was used widely in rural churches in England. It was emphasized that this new Church of the Holy Trinity would be a "free church," since pew-owning had been a controversy in Christ Church Episcopal for many years.

Tulip Street United Methodist Church
Nashville

This church was organized in 1859, but the construction of its first building was interrupted by the Civil War. After the hostilities, the church experienced steady growth, and the present unusual building was completed in 1891 at Russell and Sixth Streets.

In Romanesque Revival style, this red brick church displays fine terra cotta decorations on the exterior. A vaulted oak ceiling, reminiscent of New England churches, highlights the sanctuary, along with wood decoration which is hand carved. The chandeliers are original and the carillon chimes, installed in 1897, were made in Cincinnati and used at the Tennessee Centennial Exposition.

On March 22, 1916, a fire devastated large areas of East Nashville, but Tulip Street Church was not damaged. Again on March 14, 1933, when a tornado destroyed other buildings in the area, the church was spared.

Today, the church continues its traditions by helping the East Nashville Cooperative Ministry in providing food, clothing, medical help and ancillary services to the poor.

Holy Trinity Episcopal, Nashville

Holy Trinity was seized during the Civil War and used as a powder magazine for three months while Federal teamsters were quartered in Middle Tennessee. The altar was used for a meat cutting board and the baptismal font as a wash basin. The whole interior of the church was abused. The organ was torn to pieces, stained glass windows were smashed, and the floors were badly damaged.

When the war was over the government paid about $1300 to help rebuild the church. Christ Church and the Church of the Advent donated a carpet, an organ and chancel windows. Among the extant treasures of Holy Trinity Church are ten memorial stained glass windows, the original red cedar altar, and the elaborately carved frontal.

Holy Trinity Church is perhaps the finest example of English Country Gothic architecture in the United States and has been visited and studied by students of art and architecture for years.

Saint George's Episcopal, Nashville

Saint George's Episcopal
Nashville

In 1929, Bishop James M. Maxim, former rector of Christ Church Episcopal in Nashville and co-adjutor of the Diocese of Tennessee, and Reverend Edmund P. Dandridge, rector of Christ Church, named a committee to study the feasibility of establishing an Episcopal Church in the Belle Meade area.

The Great Depression of the thirties and World War II in the forties interrupted the activities of many major building projects. The new church was postponed until December 1944, when William H. Lambert was made chairman of the committee and given responsibility for developing a serious program for church expansion.

On May 27, 1947, Reverend Peyton R. Williams announced an anonymous gift of land on which a church was later erected. The donors were Mr. and Mrs. Brownlee O. Currey, who lived in the large French style house on the hill above the property donated. The Greek Revival chapel was built without delay, with Donald Southgate as the architect and W. F. Holt and Sons as contractors.

The cornerstone was laid on Sunday, October 20, 1949, with officiants Reverend Peyton R. Williams, Bishop Dandridge, Bishop Coadjutor Barth and Reverend Mr. Mitchell, who became vicar at the end of the service. Into the cornerstone were placed a Bible, a Prayerbook, and other documents. Saint George's became a parish in January 1952.

A new church of Greek Revival architecture is nearing completion beside the chapel, which will become the parish hall when the new church is completed.

Saint Paul's A. M. E. Church
Nashville

The plan of this building, constructed in 1870, remains unchanged, although in 1914 a new facade was added incorporating a mixture of architectural styles—Gothic, Romanesque, and early Twelfth Century Neo-Classical, with corbelling and a parapet.

This African Methodist Episcopal church was organized in 1863 under the leadership of Bishop Daniel Payne, who petitioned military governor Andrew Johnson for permission to organize a church. Under his leadership, a group from Capers Chapel became Saint John's A.M.E. Church and Andrews Chapel became Saint Paul's A.M.E.

Saint Paul's is thus one of the two oldest A.M.E. churches in the city. It has been active in community service projects and has been host to several statewide conventions.

Saint Paul's A.M.E., Nashville

Cofer's Chapel Free Will Baptist, Nashville

Cofer's Chapel Free Will Baptist Church
Nashville

This church was organized in 1880 in the home of William T. Trotter and was named in honor of the first pastor, Thomas C. Cofer.

The congregation worshipped for a time in Civil War barracks where Buena Vista School is now located. Their first building was located on Arthur Street in North Nashville, and later they moved to a building on Tenth Street.

Early pastors were George W. Binkley, John L. Welch, Sr., John S. Defoe, and John L. Welch, Jr., who served the church nearly fifty years.

The present church on King's Lane is built of brick on a nine-acre tract of land. Of vernacular Classical design, it features a graceful steeple. The congregation numbers four hundred members, who are engaged in many benevolent activities in the community.

Saint Mary's Catholic Church
Nashville

Saint Mary's church was dedicated in 1847 as the first permanent Catholic Church in Tennessee.

The first priest in Middle Tennessee, Reverend Robert Abell, was ordained in 1818 on the Eve of the Feast of the Assumption in Bardstown, Kentucky. He was described as "a powerful man physically and mentally, an orator, and a man worthy of the trust placed in him." The first Catholic Mass in Tennessee was offered to a handful of Catholics in Nashville on May 11, 1821, by Reverend Abell.

When the first bridge across the Cumberland River at Nashville was begun by the Pittsburg Company in 1824, Irish Catholic workers were brought here for the project. These workers were disappointed to arrive finding neither priest nor church. Fortunately, the generous people in other denominations contributed money for a lot to build a Catholic house of worship.

A small brick and stone building was erected, largely by the bridge builders, on Campbell's Hill (modern Capitol Hill). After the bridge was finished and most of the Catholic workers and their families returned home, the church was abandoned and fell into a bad state of repair. For many years, the only area services were held in the homes of Catholics during the biennial visits of Father Durbin of Kentucky.

In 1837, when the Third Council of Baltimore convened, Reverend Richard Pius Miles was consecrated as the first Bishop of Nashville in Bardstown, Kentucky on September 16, 1838. He arrived in Nashville to assume his duties, accompanied by Father Durbin, during the Christmas season of 1838.

In 1844 construction began on a cathedral; the pioneer church on Capitol Hill became a hospital administered by the Sisters of Charity. Part of the building was destroyed by fire in 1856, and the remaining materials were used in construction of the Church of the Assumption.

William Strickland, architect of the Tennessee State Capitol, designed the new church. Like the Capitol, it is built in Greek Revival style, with a cupola based on the monument of Lysicrates. Strickland said that Saint Mary's was his finest ecclesiastical building.

Bishop Miles died in 1860, and is buried beneath the altar in Saint Mary's. During the Civil War, when the church was used as a hospital, Bishop James Whelan ministered to the armies of both sides and in the process ruined his health. He retired after the war.

In 1914 the Cathedral of the Incarnation was built on West End, and Saint Mary's became a parish church attended from the cathedral. Among the attending priests was Chancellor Samuel Stritch, who later became Cardinal Archbishop of Chicago.

In 1925, Saint Mary's, again a regular parish, was renovated; the north and south sides were veneered with brick, the front finished with stone, and a new high altar of Botticino marble installed.

Although the furnishings have been renovated many times through the years, the basic interior design, including the elaborate ceiling moldings, remains unchanged. The church was placed on the National Register of Historic Places in 1970.

Saint Mary's Catholic, Nashville

Immanuel Baptist, Nashville

Immanuel Baptist Church
Nashville

After fifteen years as a mission Sunday School of First Baptist Church, Immanuel Baptist became an organized church on December 12, 1887.

The group met in a rent-free building at Gay and West Park Streets, then in a government-owned building on Stonewall Street, now Fifteenth Avenue South, near the state prison. Episcopal, Presbyterian and Methodist groups had met in that building in their formative years, and the Baptist mission worshipped there for eight years. In 1883 they moved into a small brick chapel on Stonewall at Hayes Street and there, in 1887, Immanuel Baptist Church was founded.

With forty-four members, Immanuel Church purchased a lot on the corner of Seventeenth and West End Avenues. A building was erected on the corner of Seventeenth and Broad in 1913. The sanctuary no longer stands, but the educational building became the Whitehall Office Building.

This sanctuary, built in the form of an equilateral cross, featured a baptistry copied from one seen in a church in Europe by Pastor Rufus W. Weaver. It resembled a sarcophagus and had a marble front.

The character of the neighborhood changed, the business district expanded and the families whom this congregation served were living a great distance from the church. In 1954 Immanuel Baptist moved to the present location on Belle Meade Boulevard. Of Greek revival architecture, this building is the work of Mr. Edwin Keeble, Nashville architect.

This church is honored in having among their members R. Lane Easterly, a descendant of of early Baptist leader Tidence Lane, and his family.

Woodmont Baptist Church
Nashville

This church was organized August 3, 1941, at Hillsboro High School, where the congregation worshipped for three years, awaiting the completion of their first meeting house. Dr. G. Allen West became the first pastor in 1941 and remained until 1967, when he was succeeded by Dr. Bill Sherman, the current pastor.

Built of brick, this Gothic building is a departure from traditional Baptist architecture. A tower between the chapel and sanctuary was included in the original plan and will be added at some time in the future.

Woodmont Church has assisted in the organization of Brook Hollow, Brentwood, Crievewood, Forest Hills, and Glenwood Churches.

Woodmont Baptist, Nashville

Brookmeade Congregational Church
Nashville

Organized as Collegeside Congregational Church in 1928 on the Peabody-Vanderbilt campus, this small company of faculty, students and friends later changed the name to Brookmeade and moved to the present location in 1954.

The present building of Neoclassical architecture was dedicated on March 4, 1982, and replaced a building which burned.

This church, which traces its beginnings to the Cambridge Platform of 1648, grew in numbers as Germans settled in Pennsylvania early in the eighteenth century and Reformed groups from Switzerland arrived in the years that followed.

Native Americans, Afro-Americans, Asian-Americans, Volga Germans, Armenians, Hispanic-Americans and Hungarians have affiliated themselves with the Congregational Church over a long period of time.

Brookmeade Church participates in the Second Harvest Food Bank and the Heifer International Project, as well as the Salvation Army Food Run.

Brookmeade Congregational, Nashville

'irst Seventh-Day Adventist Church 'ashville

. Seventh-Day Adventist congregation was active in Iashville as early as 1897, when Elder and Mrs. .ouis Hansen of Battle Creek, Michigan, arrived ere.

A small group who was meeting in an upstairs oom of the Southern Publishing Association on the orner of Warren and Jefferson Streets purchased a aptist church building on the corner of Fifth and atherland Streets for five thousand dollars. They amed it Fatherland Street Memorial Seventh-Day .dventist Church.

The Fatherland Street Church was later replaced y a small brick building on the same site. In 1947, . L. Pingenot of Battle Creek became pastor. He ad experience in church building, and soon a uilding program was initiated. On May 18, 1952, round was broken for the present building of ıodern church design. The dedication service was eld on May 1, 1954. Handsome stained glass ,indows are a prominent feature of this church.

First Seventh Day Adventist, Nashville

'ine Street Christian Church Iashville

'his church traces its history to 1820, when Baptists, lready established in Middle Tennessee, formed a hurch in Nashville. When Phillip Fall, "the Father f the Christian Church in the South," became pastor f First Baptist in 1826, he initiated several reforms ssociated with the movement known as Campbellism."

On May 24, 1828, a resolution was passed repealing all church rules and ordinances and accepting the New Testament as the sole guide for government and practice. Although the name change did not occur until later, this act may be considered as establishing the Christian Church in Nashville. At that time the congregation numbered 218, over half of whom were Black.

Alexander Campbell had a close relationship with this church, as his daughter married A. G. Ewing, an active member whose father had donated the site for the church building on Spring Street. Campbell visited Nashville in 1827, 1830, and again in 1835, when he found a congregation of six hundred.

With the appointment of Jesse B. Ferguson in 1847, the congregation began a period of growth; in 1852 a new church was built on Cherry Street. Soon dissention came, however, due to Ferguson's interest in Universalism and Spiritualism. In 1857 Ferguson resigned and the congregation scattered; only 56 remained of the previous 800 members. On April 8, 1857, the Cherry Street church burned.

Again under the leadership of Phillip Fall, the congregation bought their old building back from the Presbyterians and began to rebuild. In 1859 a separate church was established for Black members. First called Grapevine Church, then Second Christian, later Gay-Lea Christian Church, this congregation was one of the first in Nashville to possess a pipe organ.

The Nashville Christian Church continued its work during the Civil War, when many congregations were dispossessed and disorganized. Military Governor Andrew Johnson required ministers to sign a loyalty oath; many were imprisoned for refusing. Fall insisted that he had taken an oath to the Union when he became an American citizen, but Johnson maintained that this oath was invalid, as it had been taken before secession. Fall replied that if the oath was invalid, he was still a British subject.

Johnson acknowledged that he had no jurisdiction over British subjects, and Fall was allowed to continue his ministry. The British flag flew above the Christian Church, which was open to other congregations during the occupation. Fall left the pastorate in 1876, after fifty years in the ministry.

In 1889 a beautiful new church on Vine Street was completed; by the mid-twentieth century, however, most of the congregation had moved outside the downtown area. A church was established in Donelson, and the remainder of the congregation moved to a new building on Harding Road but kept the name Vine Street Christian Church.

The present Colonial church on Harding Road features a tall steeple, a unique window treatment of clear glass and weathered oak woodwork. There is also a balcony on the front of the steeple, unusual in Tennessee churches.

Long committed to a strong mission program—many early Christian and Church of Christ congregations in Middle Tennessee were organized by pastors supplied by the Nashville church—Vine Street Christian has continued its outreach with programs for prisoners and alcoholics, and with emergency aid for the needy. In addition, it has been at the center of ecumenical activity in the city.

Vine Street Christian, Nashville

Westminster Presbyterian Church
Nashville

On August 5, 1872, ground was broken for Moore Memorial Presbyterian Church at 1507-9 Broad Street, one year after the death of Dr. Thomas Verner Moore, for whom the church was named. Not yet approved by the Presbytery, this new congregation had the support of First Presbyterian Church of Nashville, where Dr. Moore had succeeded

Westminster Presbyterian, Nashville

Dr. Robert F. Bunting as pastor.

Dr. Moore had served as pastor of First Presbyterian Church in Richmond, Virginia, and was Moderator of the General Assembly of the Presbyterian Church in the United States when that body met in Nashville in 1867. He was known for his advocacy of establishing churches in neglected areas and was instrumental in the organization of Moore Memorial Church. He died in 1871.

Through the efforts of five young women, a Sunday School began meeting in a small building at the rear of the home of Captain J. W. Fulcher. It was one of several such buildings erected by the government during the Union occupation. The Sunday School began three months after the death of Dr. Moore, with George O'Bryan as superintendent. He served for twenty-five years.

Moore Memorial Presbyterian was organized as a church on November 23, 1873, in the Lecture Room of First Presbyterian. Reverend Frank D. Moore, son of Dr. Thomas Verner Moore, became the first pastor. Twenty-two years old when his father died, young Frank Moore was not a member of the church and had studied law.

In June 1872 a building lot was built on Broad Street opposite Fifteenth Street, and on March 22, 1874, the new Moore Memorial Presbyterian Church was dedicated and the new pastor, Reverend Frank D. Moore, delivered the sermon.

Mr. Earl Swensson, an architect and elder at this church, described it as "eclectic Victorian." It featured a single steeple at the side of the building, with onion minarets of Byzantine design. Windows and doorways were Gothic and the brick patterns in the outer walls were of Romanesque design.

In 1934 plans for a new church were being made, and the site on which Westminster Church stands today was purchased. The firm of Warfield and Keeble, architects, was engaged to design and build the new church.

Groundbreaking was held on October 30, 1937, with the first spade of dirt being moved by Miss Mattie Thompson, who at eighty-seven years of age was the only living charter member of Moore Memorial Church.

The last worship service was held in the old building on September 3, 1937. The first service in the new church, whose name had been changed to Westminster Presbyterian Church, was held in that building of Colonial architecture on September 10, 1937.

Christ Church Pentecostal
Nashville

This congregation was organized in 1949 by Reverend J. O. Wallace, who established several churches in Middle Tennessee. Its original building was located at the corner of Rose and Sadler Streets in Woodbine.

In 1950, Reverend L. H. Hardwick became pastor at age eighteen. He is still pastor in 1986, having served this church for thirty-six years.

A new site was selected on Elberta Street in Woodbine, and the church basement was completed in 1957. The congregation met here until the sanctuary, with a capacity of 250, was completed in 1963.

The church moved to five acres on Old Hickory Boulevard in 1977, and completed the present building there the following year. It is a modern design, featuring a mansard roof, created by architect Bill Shelton. Christ Church now owns thirty acres on this site, and an extensive building program is underway.

Present membership is between eight and nine hundred, including a nationally known choir which contains professional musicians. A major international Bible Conference meets here annually.

Christ Church Pentecostal, Nashville

West End Church of Christ
Nashville

This congregation became a church in 1927 and erected a building in 1956. Greek Revival architecture is reflected in the present buildings, and the sanctuary was the first house of worship in Nashville to be fully air-conditioned.

West End Church of Christ, Nashville

Woodmont Christian Church
Nashville

Woodmont Christian Church was organized in a meeting at Woodmont School on July 18, 1943, with fifty-one members. Soon a four story red brick colonial house was purchased on the corner of Woodmont Boulevard and Hillsboro Road; this building was for a time used as sanctuary, Sunday School, church office, and parsonage.

In 1947, ground was broken for the new sanctuary, which was was built by contractor W. D. Gardner. Gardner was not at the time a member of the church, but was later one of the first to be baptized in the new building.

The beautiful white brick sanctuary, reminiscent of old New England church design, was completed in 1949. Its 220 foot tall spire is a landmark in the Hillsboro area.

Woodmont Christian, Nashville

Capers Memorial C.M.E., Nashville

Gay-Lea Christian, Nashville

Gay-Lea Christian Church Nashville

This church traces its origins to 1824, when the first Black Sunday School in Nashville was organized by First Christian Church. By 1849 there was a separate congregation, and in 1850 Elder Peter Lowery became the first minister. In 1859 this congregation became Grapevine Church and met in the pastor's home.

In 1866 the church moved to its own building on Vine Street and attained complete independence from the White congregation; records refer to it as both First Colored Christian and Second Christian Church. It later moved to Gay Street and took the name Gay Street Christian. This church was one of the first in Nashville to have a pipe organ.

Preston Taylor, pastor of Gay Street Christian, was an early leader in the struggle for Black rights. He organized the Nashville streetcar boycott, and left most of the assets of his funeral home to the National Christian Missionary Association. In 1886, he left the Gay Street church and organized Lea Avenue Christian.

Later the two congregations merged and formed Gay-Lea Christian Church. The present building on Osage Avenue was erected in 1957.

Capers Memorial C. M. E. Church Nashville

Capers Memorial Church traces its origins from the African Mission of McKendree Methodist, begun in 1832. In 1851 the congregation moved to their own building on Hynes street, which was called Capers Chapel in honor of their founder, Bishop Capers.

In 1863, Bishop Payne came to Nashville to organize Black Methodist groups into the independent A.M.E. denomination. Andrews Chapel became Saint Paul's A.M.E. Church, and a group from Capers Chapel became Saint John's A.M.E. in 1865, with Napoleon Merry, a noted A.M.E. leader, as pastor.

Capers Memorial Church was organized in 1867 and soon affiliated with the Colored (now Christian) Methodist Episcopal Church.

The present building on Fifth Avenue North is one of the first church designs of the noted architectural firm of McKissack and McKissack. The Neoclassic church is virtually unaltered from its original 1925 appearance and has been placed on the National Register of Historic Places.

Woodland Presbyterian, Nashville

Woodland Presbyterian
Nashville

In 1858, colonies of ten persons each from First and Second Presbyterian Churches organized Edgefield Presbyterian Church. Their first building was erected in 1859, and was replaced in 1887 by a structure of the vernacular Gothic church architecture typical of the period in Edgefield.

The second church burned in 1916 and was replaced by the present building, completed in 1917 and dedicated November 11, 1918. This Neoclassical church, in which both Greek and Roman influences can be seen, was designed by W. Terrill Hall and features beautiful colored windows and interesting ceiling plaster work. An exquisitely crafted quilt depicting church history hangs in the hall behind the sanctuary.

The name was changed to Woodland Street Presbyterian in 1889 and to Woodland Presbyterian in 1946. Today the church is active in many community services through the East Nashville Cooperative Ministry.

Edgefield Baptist
Nashville

Edgefield Baptist was organized with thirty-one members, many of whom had withdrawn from First Baptist for the purpose, on April 14, 1867. The Ladies' Sewing Circle, which at the time paid half of the church's operating expenses, was organized the following day.

The church met in Stubb's (Masonic) Hall until 1873, when the first building was erected. This building was sold and replaced by the present structure, completed in 1907. The first contribution recorded for this building was $3.75 from Jennie Averitt, who earned it by "being a good girl and taking her medicine" while she was sick.

Plans for the building were drawn by Wheeler, Runge, and Dickey, of the vernacular red brick Gothic style favored in Edgefield at the time. Beautiful memorial stained glass windows depicting "Jesus Walking on the Water" and "The Good Shepherd" face Russell and Seventh Streets.

The 1,050-voice Moller pipe organ was installed in 1907, due in part to a gift from Andrew Carnegie. This valuable instrument was rebuilt in 1972.

The church was saved from the 1916 Edgefield fire by the earnest efforts of a fire department bucket brigade. In 1933, a tornado damaged the tower, which was rebuilt in a shorter version due to new city regulations.

Several former pastors of Edgefield Baptist have become denominational leaders; the church has provided four missionary secretaries for three different state conventions. The Nashville Baptist Association was organized here on July 23, 1900.

Edgefield Baptist, Nashville

First Baptist Church, Capitol Hill
Nashville

As early as 1843 Black members of First Baptist Church of Nashville were organized into a separate congregation, which moved in 1849 into its own building on Pearl Street and later into a new facility on Spruce Street. The church achieved independence from the White congregation in 1864.

Much of the credit for organizing this congregation goes to its first Black pastor, Nelson Merry. As a slave, he had been willed to the church by his mistress and served for many years as sexton and caretaker before becoming pastor in 1852. Merry became a respected leader in Nashville, and his funeral in 1884 was attended by people from both the Black and White communities.

In 1887, leadership conflicts resulted in a split in the congregation; one group remained in the church building and became Spruce Street Baptist, while another kept the name First Baptist Church and relocated to Eighth Avenue North. Relations became cordial between the churches, which later cooperated in community service efforts. The name of First Baptist was changed to First Baptist Church, Capitol Hill in 1965.

No history of First Baptist would be complete without reference to Reverend Kelly Miller Smith, pastor of the church from 1952 until his death in 1984, and for a time a dean of the Vanderbilt Divinity School. Under Dr. Smith, the church had an active ministry of social concerns and a summer school program for church and community youth, and began a 110-unit highrise apartment building for the elderly. Like Nelson Merry, Kelly Miller Smith was a strong and respected leader of the Black community.

First Baptist Church, Capitol Hill, Nashville

Russell Street Church of Christ, Nashville

Russell Street Church of Christ
Nashville

A Church of Christ congregation was organized in Edgefield with nineteen members on October 26, 1890. Among the first elders were William Lipscomb, Sr. and E. G. Sewell. The congregation met in schoolrooms until a small house was purchased on Tenth Street.

By 1898 the congregation had grown so much that a lot was purchased and a church built at Russell and Tenth Streets; in 1913, this church was exchanged for the present building, which had been owned by Cumberland Presbyterians.

This Romanesque revival building contains beautiful stained glass windows which may have come from Tiffany. Unusual brickwork archways frame the doors.

Belmont Heights Baptist Church
Nashville

On May 2, 1920, members of Southside Baptist Church on Belcourt Avenue and Belmont Baptist Church on Twelfth Avenue South voted to merge and take the name Belmont Heights Baptist Church. The congregation met first in the Ward Belmont College auditorium and later under a tent on a lot north of Sterling Court. The first church building was begun in 1923 and completed in 1926; the present auditorium was built in 1956.

On March 26, 1933, during the worst of the depression, an offering of old gold and silver was collected to help pay Cooperative Program debts. A total of 119 rings, 45 watches, 48 spoons, 98 links and studs, 76 chains, 57 pins and $7.10 in cash was collected.

Belmont Heights has long provided services for students at Belmont College, and has been at the forefront in providing services in foreign languages. A Korean mission was begun in 1966 and a separate Korean congregation established in 1976. A Laotian ministry was started in 1980 and Cambodian and Chinese ministries in 1981.

Many state and regional conferences have been held at Belmont Heights, and at least eight other churches or missions have been started by this congregation. In 1986, a new Family Life Center was dedicated to strengthen church programs and outreach to the community.

Belmont Heights Baptist, Nashville

Concord Baptist, Nolensville

Concord Baptist Church
Nolensville

Elder James Whitsett organized Mill Creek Church, the first Baptist congregation in Davidson County, on April 15, 1797, and became its first pastor. It was here that the first Tennessee Baptist Convention was organized in 1833.

In September 1812, Whitsett founded the Concord Association in the Concord Primitive Baptist meeting house in Nolensville. This congregation had been organized by Garner McConico and Joshua White on August 11, 1804, with 142 members, and was the forerunner of Concord Baptist.

Dissention occurred in the Concord church, as in the denomination at large, over the question of centralization of authority. A group led by William H. Nance was expelled in 1835 and took with them the record book. In 1836, the Concord Association was dissolved over the same issue, and Concord Church, led by James Whitsett, joined the new Stones River Association, from which grew the General Association of the Baptists of Tennessee.

In 1842, the church determined that the old meetinghouse was unsatisfactory and began the process of preparing to build a new one under the leadership of William A. Whitsett. A grandson of James Whitsett, William was ordained as deacon in 1842 and as pastor in 1844; he served for over twenty years and was a mainstay of the church until his death in 1883.

In 1844, the "Old Confession of Faith" was rejected by the congregation, and a new statement of faith was adopted which reflected the sentiments of the congregation and placed them firmly in the camp of the Missionary or United Baptists, out of which grew the Southern Baptist Church of today. This change, however, necessitated giving up the old meeting house, in which a Primitive Baptist group worshipped until at least 1860.

The current Concord Baptist Church was built on a nearby site in 1845 and continues as an active church today. The simple brick meeting house has had additions built to the front and rear but still forms the core of the building. An unusual brick molding can be seen at the edge of the roof of the older structure.

Mount Olivet Methodist, Nolensville

Mount Olivet Methodist Church
Nolensville

According to tradition, Mount Olivet was organized in Nolensville in 1837 with 37 members. A log building with a brick foundation and puncheon floor was built soon after; it was replaced by a frame church in 1858. The congregation was part of a charge which included Triune and Hebron.

The present building was begun in 1894 and completed in 1897. A Mr. Ezell from Antioch served as contractor, but members of the congregation donated labor and supplies to aid in completing construction.

The church was heated by wood stoves until the late 1940's, when a coal furnace was installed. The basement and additional rooms were added below the sanctuary in the 1930's, the 1950's, and again in 1976.

This vernacular Gothic building contains several memorial windows and features a graceful seventy-five foot steeple.

First Baptist Church
Paris

Six women and four men met in the home of one of the group in Paris on August 29, 1833, and organized the First Baptist Church of Paris.

A one-fourth acre lot in the southwest corner of the town was purchased, and two years later a frame church with wide plank floors was completed in January 1836 at a cost of $342.

Minutes reveal that the congregation met for worship at the church on the first "Saturday and Sunday of each month. Sabbath morning at Noterside." The minutes also state that baptisms took place at the Harris Mill at North Poplar Street, and that the first lighting system was "candles at twelve and a half per month," and later "lamp oil, fifty cents per month."

In August 1883, the land on which the church stood was sold. The church and its furnishings and appointments were retained, and later the building was disposed of and furnishings used in the new church. This building, dedicated in 1890, was of red brick and stood on ground now occupied by Sunday School rooms.

Another building was built in 1905 of grey brick, and the present Greek Revival church was dedicated on May 27, 1923.

First Baptist, Paris

Grace Episcopal Church
Paris

This is the oldest church building in Paris, consecrated on November 10, 1895, by Bishop Thomas F. Gailor.

In February 1854, Reverend Mr. Gray, later Bishop of Florida, rode from Bolivar to Paris and was so cold and stiff he had to be assisted off his horse. He preached a sermon in the Henry County courthouse that night to a few citizens. Although some people, chiefly women, were interested in organizing an Episcopal Church, no effort was made to establish one until 1894.

A site was purchased, other land was donated, and the building was completed and free of debt by November 1904. Money was raised in many ways, and financier J. P. Morgan donated $250 for the roof.

The large window over the altar was designed and created at the Tiffany factory in Versailles, France. Records state that pieces of the window were wrapped in straw, shipped in wooden kegs to

Grace Episcopal, Paris

Philadelphia, and taken by horse-drawn wagon to Lancaster, Pennsylvania, where the window was assembled by the Berghause Company. When completed, the window was suspended on a steel rod in a vertical position, moved by horse-drawn wagon to Pittsburgh, then sent to Paris on a flatcar. Five days were required for installation in 1895, and the total cost was $1,800.

The large rose windows in the west end of the church were replaced in 1966 and dedicated to the memory of Mrs. Margaret W. Travathan by her children. These windows were made of shards gathered from cathedrals in Europe which were destroyed in the two World Wars. Some of these pieces date from the fifteenth century.

First United Methodist, Paris

First United Methodist Church Paris

In November 1831, in a rough-hewn log mission chapel, Bishop Joshua Soule, presiding over the Tennessee Annual Conference, declared the Methodist Church in Paris to be a station.

Carefully preserved records, written with a quill pen and home made ink, show that Reverend G.W.D. Harris, brother of Governor Isham G. Harris, was the presiding elder here in 1831, and Reverend Phineas T. Scruggs was pastor. A different pastor each year was the custom until 1837 when Dr. Wesley Warren, doctor and minister, served two years.

In 1853, a new brick church was erected, and a balcony was built on each of the inside walls for the use of slaves of the members. In 1858-59, Reverend Lewis H. Davis, a blind minister, served as pastor, constantly attended by a Black servant named Billy Davis.

The church was badly damaged during the Civil War, and the records mention meeting with other denominations while a new building was being erected. That new church was damaged by fire in 1873 and required extensive repairs.

In 1860, a melodeon, little more than two feet wide, was purchased and Mrs. F.F. Porter, the former Miss Willie Burgess, played the instrument for worship, while Marcellus Rison sat beside her to manipulate the foot pedal bellows and direct singing.

The Annual Conference met in Paris again in 1902 and the church burned on April 1, 1903. On April 17, 1904, a new church was dedicated. Bishop Boaz preached the first sermon in the present church in 1926.

Church of the Messiah, Episcopal Pulaski

Located in Pulaski, this one-story brick church was built in 1887 in the style of a nineteenth century English parish church. Rectangular in shape, the building measures thirty-eight by sixty feet.

The interior, still original, features brick walls, dark woodwork, a central aisle flanked by wooden pews, and an elaborately carved Gothic reredos.

Architect George W. Quintard, son of Bishop Charles Todd Quintard, designed the church and supervised the construction. Sullivan and Woodring were the stonecutters, and S. C. Mitchell was the contractor. The money for the building, amounting to $6000, was donated by Governor John C. Brown and his wife in memory of two deceased daughters.

The dedication of the Church of the Messiah was held in December 1887, and was attended by Governor Brown and his wife, Bishop Quintard of Tennessee, Bishop Pierce of Arkansas, Bishop Garrett of Northern Texas, and Reverend Thomas F. Gailor, later Bishop of Tennessee.

Church of the Messiah, Episcopal, Pulaski

First United Methodist Church
Pulaski

A church called Richland was organized in Pulaski in 1810 or sooner, before Pulaski was chartered as a town, and before President James Madison made a land grant of six hundred and forty acres to the commissioners of Pulaski in 1811.

According to tradition, the first church, located at the end of South Third Street, was built of logs and measured eighteen by twenty feet. A frame structure replaced it on a lot near the county jail on South First Street. A third building was a beautiful brick church at 302 North Second Street which was sold to the Church of Christ in 1851.

The present impressive Gothic church, with a handsome tower and stained glass of cathedral quality, was first occupied in 1901. The name became First United Methodist Church some time later.

Leaner Blackman, the Presiding Elder serving this church from 1811 to 1814, was chosen by Andrew Jackson as chaplain in the War of 1812 and was with him in New Orleans. Dr. James B. McFerrin was the first pastor after this church became a station in 1834.

First United Methodist, Pulaski

First Presbyterian Church
Pulaski

Among the earliest settlers in Giles County was a band of Scotch-Irish Presbyterians. As early as 1812, a request was sent to the Presbytery of West Tennessee for supplies. Although Reverend Gideon Blackburn preached in the area, no church was formed for sixteen years.

The Presbyterian Church in Pulaski was officially organized on July 12, 1828. The first pastor was Reverend James Hall Brookes, who had arrived in the Spring of that year as head of the Female Academy.

First Presbyterian, Pulaski

In 1825, two lots were purchased at the corner of Third and Washington Streets for a church site, and a two story building was erected. This first building was owned jointly by the Masonic Lodge, Old Presbyterians, and Cumberland Presbyterians.

Sentiments in favor of a new church were voiced in 1851. Part of a lot at the corner of Flower and Second Streets was purchased, and the Masonic Lodge bought the interest in the old building held by the Presbyterian congregation. Work started on a new church in 1853, and in 1855 worship was begun in the unfinished building.

Dr. William Stoddert, pastor in 1865, was born in Virginia to Dr. Thomas Ewell and Elizabeth Stoddert Ewell. William was the grandson of Benjamin Stoddert, first Secretary of the United States Navy, and, at the request of his mother, changed his name legally from Ewell to Stoddert. Reverend James Cake Mitchell, born James Mitchell Cake in Norfolk, Virginia, also took his mother's maiden name.

The third and present church of this congregation at Second and Flower Streets was dedicated May 3, 1885. This Romanesque-Gothic church of red brick features a vaulted ceiling and much stained glass. Handsome carving decorating the ends of the pews was supervized by Deacon Caleb Osborn.

Many memorials have been placed in this church, including a silver communion service and a portable service for the sick and shut-ins, an iconograph executed by Bill Heaton, a four-foot gold cross over the organ console, a gold cross in the chapel, tall silver vases used on special occasions, hymn books, altar hangings, and a handmade lectern and baptismal font.

First Presbyterian, Pulaski (detail)

Immanuel Lutheran, Reedy Creek

Immanuel Lutheran Church
Reedy Creek

One of the oldest Lutheran congregations in Tennessee, Immanuel traces its origins to the Old Union Church, founded in 1785. This church had a hewn-log and puncheon construction and was replaced in 1810 by a frame structure with an open fireplace at one end.

A third building was constructed of brick in 1865 and replaced by another brick building in 1903, to which an education wing has been added.

Bricks for the church were made by members of the congregation. Topsoil was stripped from a field and clay removed; this clay was pulverized by a horse-powered mixer, and water was added. The resulting thick mud was pressed into molds and dipped in sand for glazing, dried on the ground, and baked in kilns.

livet United Methodist, Riverburg

)livet United Methodist Church
Riverburg

This church, built in 1871 in the northern part of the ounty, features elaborate "gingerbread" decoration.)livet Station School, built in 1893, is located on the ame property, along with the parsonage, built in 900. Of frame construction, these buildings are onsidered outstanding examples of Victorian /ernacular Chapel Architecture.

The land on which this complex stands was deeded o the Olivet Methodist Church by Colonel David T. Reynolds and Albert Buford. Construction of the hurch was financed by Colonel Reynolds. Dr. Alexander L. P. Green preached the dedication sermon, and Reverend J. B. Anderson became the first pastor. There were eighteen charter members.

During the 1920's "Children's Day" became an annual occasion here. Children would march into the church in long lines singing "Onward Christian Soldiers," followed by songs, recitations, dramas, duets and solos. Ladies of the church carried ferns, wild roses, sweet peas, lilies, and Queen Anne's Lace.

The church was moved approximately one hundred feet from its original location when the highway claimed a portion of the front lawn.

Mount Zion Methodist, Robertson County

Mount Zion Methodist Church
Robertson County

In 1798, Mount Zion Methodist Church was organized in the home of Samuel Crockett, a veteran of the Revolutionary War and a leader in Robertson County. This remote congregation, the oldest in Robertson County, worshipped in the homes of settlers in the area until 1804, when a small house was built for them on a two-acre lot donated by Thomas and Patrick Martin.

A second building here blew away in a storm in 1844, and the present church of vernacular Middle Tennessee architecture of the period was erected in 1883 on the same site.

A large campground was maintained here, and an old cemetery adjacent to the church grounds is enclosed by a wall believed to have been built by Benjamin Menees, Jr., an early settler who fought with Andrew Jackson in the Creek Indian War and the War of 1812.

First Baptist Church
Rogersville

William Cate, a missionary of the Southern Baptist Board, organized this church on December 20, 1852. With Noah Cate as pastor, the group worshipped in the Presbyterian and Methodist Churches while their own church was being built on Depot Street adjacent to the Shank Hotel. It was completed in 1853, but was burned during the Civil War.

Rogersville Baptist Church was reorganized in 1890, and the present Greek Revival building was erected that year. Reverend J. C. Chiles, a well-known minister in the area, served as pastor for thirty years, and records show that he baptized 776 people during his pastorate. Five mission churches were organized under his leadership.

First Baptist, Rogersville

ethesda Presbyterian Church
amblen County

his simple brick church has stood beside an old metery in a grove of trees since 1835. Elder oseph Shannon donated three and one half acres of nd for a church in 1834, and the building was mpleted the next year.

The church was organized in 1832 by Rev. John IcCampbell. Dr. Nathaniel Hood became the first astor, and served until 1844. The Reverend enjamin Lee was the last pastor here, and the nurch became inactive in 1871.

This building became a Confederate hospital uring the Civil War. In 1878, the church's few emaining members were granted letters and were ee to become members elsewhere.

The building and grounds are still in good ondition, and occasionally a funeral is held there.

ethesda Presbyterian, Russellville

Old Russellville Methodist Church
Russellville

Built in 1832, this church with two front doors—one for men, one for women—was built of hand-made brick fired nearby, and has a rich history.

Filled with sick and wounded soldiers throughout the Civil War, the basement served as a hospital for both Confederate and Union armies. Assisted by the old and infirm of the community, the women and children cared for all who sought refuge here. Often the only medicines were home remedies, teas, and herbs. These same women and children dug graves and buried the dead in the churchyard.

Old Russellville Methodist, Russellville

Beesley Church, Rutherford County

Beesley Church
Rutherford County

One of the earliest Primitive Baptist churches in Tennessee, Beesley Church still stands adjacent to land owned by lineal descendents of Elder John Beesley. This property has been in the same family for almost 200 years.

A group of families led by Solomon and John Beesley moved from North Carolina to Rutherford County in the early years of the nineteenth century; their first camp in the area was on or near the site of the church. Local tradition has it that on that first night a deer was startled by the party's dogs and leapt over the company's campfire, and John Beesley shot that deer and made a rug of the skin and hatrack of the antlers.

The church, originally called Overall Primitive Baptist Church, was organized in 1804 with John Beesley as presiding elder. By 1827 it had 154 members, but in that year Pastor Payton Smith and 54 of the members "gave up the Baptist faith for another."

The first log church was burned in 1856, and a frame building was built a few yards to the southeast. It was destroyed by a storm in 1887. The church served as a Union headquarters during the Civil War, but for some reason sustained no damage.

The first brick building on the site was destroyed by a cyclone in 1911. According to reports of the time, the building was torn from its foundation and moved almost a hundred yards from its site, facing the opposite direction. The pews, altar furniture, and communion pitchers and glasses were left undisturbed on the foundation.

The rebuilt church, still standing beneath a venerable Maple tree, was active until 1949. For many years it has been cared for by members of the Beesley family. Primitive Baptists from Rutherford and Williamson Counties have held July 4 reunions here in recent years.

The simple red brick church, typical of rural church architecture in Tennessee, has a distinctive curved stucco entryway and tall shuttered windows. In the churchyard is a cemetery with gravestones dating from 1834; many generations of the Beesleys and other pioneer families are buried here. The cemetery continues to be used by both Black and White families in the area.

Christ Church Episcopal, Rugby

Christ Church Episcopal
Rugby

On October 5, 1880, a ceremony opening Rugby Colony was held. Founder Thomas Hughes told a large crowd that the purpose of the venture was to plant a community in that place for ladies and gentlemen who could succeed by the labor of their own hands.

A former member of the British Parliament, Thomas Hughes was known on both sides of the Atlantic as the author of *Tom Brown's School Days.* His sympathies for the plight of "younger sons" of the landed English gentry led him to the presidency of the Board of Aid to Land Ownership, which sought to assist settlers by the advantageous purchase of large areas of land and the sale of it in small parcels on credit. By 1880, Hughes' company had secured 400,000 acres on the Cumberland Plateau in Tennessee.

The one hundred young men, only a few of whom brought wives, were ill-fitted for life in a rigorous wilderness. The colonists spent their time in tennis clubs, debating clubs, drama and music organizations, riding blooded horses imported from abroad, and writing articles for newspapers. They remained aloof from the native population, who avoided them as well.

A library building was erected, and Hughes collected several thousand fine books from publishers here and abroad. This library and its books are in excellent condition and are on display at Rugby.

Early in the development of the colony, Christ Church Episcopal was founded by the Right Reverend Charles Todd Quintard on October 15, 1880, in the vestibule of the Tabard Hotel. The meeting was conducted by Joseph H. Blacklock, the first priest.

While the church was being built, worship was held in the Town Hall. All work on the building was performed by a group of local artisans, using pine, oak, and walnut timber cut on the site and milled in a planing mill by the river. This original building still stands.

The dominant feature of the sanctuary is a group of three stained glass windows above the altar dedicated to the memory of Mrs. Margaret Hughes, mother of Thomas Hughes, and to Mrs. Mary Blacklock, mother of Joseph H. Blacklock. The cross-stitched kneeler was made by members of the Guild Working Society under the direction of Mrs. Hughes, and, though somewhat faded, is in good condition today.

Seventeen pews, choir stalls, and a rosewood organ made in England in 1849, given by the Blacklock family, are still in use. The organ, of melodeon type, is believed to be one of the oldest of its kind in use today.

The Church of Saint Joseph of Arimathea, Catholic Saint Joseph

The original church at Saint Joseph, built in 1872, no longer stands. The present one, built in 1885, is a large building of ashlar cut stone quarried and finished by the parishioners who built the church.

Saint Joseph contains one of the most elaborately decorated interiors of any church in the central South. Much of the interior was decorated by the Reverend John Sliemers, parish priest from 1901 to 1903, and again from 1914 until his death in 1934. While no longer an active church, this building is a historical landmark for the German Catholic community in Lawrence County.

First United Methodist Church Savannah

The Methodist Church in Savannah was formed in 1844, and a deed for a tract of land on which to build a church and parsonage was made in 1847. The church built there was used for worship until the Battle of Shiloh, just eight miles upriver from Savannah, on April 6 and 7, 1862, when it became a hospital for the Union army. Reverend W. H. Browning, pastor, entered the Confederate army and became a chaplain of the Fifty-first Infantry.

In 1870, the church was damaged by lightning, and soon afterwards the Gothic building now in use was constructed.

Hardin College in Savannah was not affiliated with any church body but maintained a close relationship with the Methodist Church. W. D. Will, son of Reverend J. C. Will, a Methodist minister, was President of Hardin College.

First United Methodist, Savannah

Saint Joseph of Arimathea, Saint Joseph

Saint Luke's Chapel
Sewanee

This small chapel near the School of Theology was a gift of Mrs. Telfair Hodgson in memory to a former dean of the Seminary. It was completed in 1904.

Built of Tennessee sandstone, as are most of the other buildings of the University, Saint Luke's chapel is designed in the style of an English Country Gothic church.

Saint Luke's Chapel, Sewanee

All Saints' Chapel
University of the South, Sewanee

In the plan of the University of the South in 1857, a chapel was listed as a future building. Nearly half a century passed before the foundations were laid for this Gothic chapel of Tennessee sandstone.

The walls were completed to the clerestory before 1910. A temporary roof was added, and the chapel was used in this unfinished state until it was finally completed in 1957.

Many treasures and memorials are found in the sanctuary. A chalice in constant use was given by Charles Minnegerode Fairbanks, Bishop of Alabama, in memory of his wife Susan, daughter of one of the founders of the University. After her death he had her wedding silver melted and and made into a chalice and paten, with her engagement diamond and wedding ring set in the chalice.

All Saints Chapel, Sewanee

The family altar from the home of Bishop Leonidas Polk in Beersheba Springs serves as the chapel altar. Before being moved to Sewanee, it was used as a stand for a water pitcher in a hotel and a meat cutting block. It was brought to the University and restored in 1950. The chair of Bishop Polk, from the Christ Church Cathedral in New Orleans, stands near the main altar.

A bell from Old Saint Augustine's chapel now hangs in Saint Luke's Tower. The Breslin Chimes, which have the same tones as the chimes in Westminster Abbey in London, England, were given in memory of Mrs. Charlotte Ferris Douglas.

William Dudley Gale III, great-grandson of Bishop Polk, remained in France for a time after World War I, and acquired an appreciation and knowledge of carrillons. He donated $65,000 the second largest gift received) toward the completion of All Saints' Chapel. The carillon was given in memory of Bishop Polk.

The largest gift to the chapel was donated by the Shapard family of Griffin, Georgia, and led to the building of the Shapard Tower, where the carillon was hung. The largest bell weighs 7,500 pounds and is inscribed "To Polk and to Sewanee, my Alma Mater, this carillon is dedicated." Seventeen other bells are dedicated to members of the donor's family.

The chapel is used for daily services of worship and the University convocations, including those at which degrees are conferred.

First United Methodist, Smyrna

First United Methodist Church
Smyrna

Records show that in October, 1872, Brother J. J. Pittman was assigned to the Smyrna charge, and he organized a Methodist church there in 1873.

On the first church roll appear the names of the family of the Confederat hero Sam Davis. The list includes grandmother Elizabeth Simmons, father Lewis Davis, Sr., mother Jane Davis, and brother Oscar Davis.

The first building was completed on the present location in 1872. That two-storied church burned. Another one was constructed on the same site, and records state that the Brown family did much of the labor. One member of the family built the chancel rail and altar of cedar and assisted with other architectural details and furniture. Mrs. Media Moore donated a "settee" for the pulpit.

In 1925, the old church was razed and the present Gothic style church was completed in 1926. Dr. W. J. Engles, who was present when the cornerstone was laid for the 1871 church, was also present when the cornerstone was unveiled for the present one in 1926.

Saint Thomas Episcopal
Somerville

Organized in 1834 by the Reverend Samuel George Litton, Saint Thomas is one of the oldest Episcopal churches in West Tennessee. Mr. Litton was born in Ireland, graduated from the University of Dublin, and was sent to the Western District by Bishop Otey.

Saint Thomas church was slow in developing a strong congregation, but in 1839 worship services were begun by the former rector of Saint Andrew's, a nearby church which had disbanded. The congregation met in the Masonic Hall until 1858, when a simple Gothic church was built. It was dedicated during the annual convention of the Tennessee diocese in Saint Thomas in May 1861. This convention was the last one held before the Civil War, and the last attended by Bishop Otey.

Many memorials have been placed in Saint Thomas Church. The window over the altar was given in memory of the Reverend Davis Sessums, Bishop of Louisiana, by his family. A window in the west wall was given in memory of Reverend John Miller Schwar, rector in 1878, who died of yellow fever in that year, and the marble cross on the altar is a memorial to his wife Anna.

Silver for the altar vessels came from members of the Ladies' Guild, and the chalice is decorated with jewels from the same ladies. The reredos was given in memory of General Joseph Williams by members of his family.

Saint Thomas Episcopal, Somerville

First United Presbyterian Church
Sparta

A Presbyterian congregation was organized soon after the town of Sparta was laid out by the first settlers in 1802. A building was constructed in 1813 which served both the church and Priestly Academy, which had been founded by Dr. Hezekiah Priestly, pastor of the church.

In 1844, the first building constructed in Sparta for exclusively religious purposes was built by the Presbyterian congregation. Records have been lost, however, for the last half of the the nineteenth century.

In 1906, a church was organized at the present location by six ladies from McMinnville. Reverend Richard H. Brown was the first minister in the new building, which was completed in 1910.

This small but handsome Gothic Revival church features an unusual octagonal tower at the entranceway. It continues to serve a small Presbyterian congregation.

First Presbyterian, Sparta

First Presbyterian Church
Shelbyville

William H. Gosling, an English immigrant, designed this two-story building in the classic Greek Revival ecclesiastical style. It was erected in 1854.

The church was organized in 1810 out of a "Society of Believers" and became a Presbyterian congregation in 1815. The first building was made of logs and stood on the corner of East Lane and North Jefferson Streets. In 1825 that building was replaced by a brick building on the same site. It is now the Church of the Redeemer, Episcopal.

In 1852 the present handsome church was erected. Used as a hospital by both Federal and Confederate troops, it appears to have functioned as a house of worship during at least part of the Civil War. Records show that a major religious revival took place here among Confederate troops in June 1863, and that Commanding General Braxton Bragg was baptized in this church during that revival.

Many interesting relics of the church are housed here, and an original bronze chandelier and stained glass windows are notable features. The "Anchor Cross" window in the sanctuary was given in memory of Mr. and Mrs. J. D. Wilhoite by their children in 1898.

First Presbyterian, Shelbyville

Big Spring Union Church
Springdale

One of the few remaining examples of frontier church architecture, Big Spring is one of the oldest churches still actively functioning in Tennessee.

The church was built in the winter of 1795-96. A local farmer, Drew Harrell, hewed the logs and, together with Reverend Tidence Lane, built the church. The minutes of 1800 state that Jesse Dodson was the first pastor.

Today, Big Spring Union Church remains in very good condition because it lies in a remote and isolated area. It was untouched even by the Civil War.

Big Spring Union Church, Springdale

Grace Episcopal Church
Spring Hill

Marked by dignity and simplicity, this white painted building of batten and board construction was designed by P.J. Williamson of Nashville and built in 1877. It features stained glass lancet windows, handsome kneelers, and a rare handcarved altar rail of solid walnut. A graceful bell tower and spire rising seventy feet is topped with a cross. The bell bears the inscription, "England, 1839."

The Pilcher organ was purchased with funds raised by Miss Gloucester, a teacher in the nearby Beechcroft School and organist here for many years. The organ has been electrified and is still in use.

At one time Grace Church enjoyed the largest attendance of any church in Spring Hill, but later that situation changed and it was feared that the church might be closed. Devout members and relatives of the Polk and Campbell families were instrumental in keeping the church open.

Today the church is more active and receives visitors each month from all over the United States and many foreign countries.

Grace Episcopal, Spring Hill

Spring Hill Presbyterian Church
Spring Hill

This congregation was organized in 1844 by Reverends Robert Garrison and Robert Hardin with twenty-six original members.

Church minutes indicate that the first building was dedicated on March 18, 1849, and it is believed that F.A. Thompson, minister of First Presbyterian Church in Franklin from 1873 to 1878, supervised the construction.

In 1888 the original building was demolished and the present frame church, of eclectic vernacular style, was constructed. Fine craftsmanship is evident throughout the interior. The pews are almost identical to those in First Presbyterian Church in Franklin.

The church is essentially unaltered from the original appearance and condition. Tongue-and-groove paneling, ash flooring and stained glass windows are used in an understated decor. Electric lighting has been installed and two recent additions to the rear of the building are not visible from the street.

Spring Hill Presbyterian

Spring Hill United Methodist Church
Spring Hill

Nathaniel Cheairs moved to Middle Tennessee in 1810 and claimed a tract of land granted to him for service in the Revolutionary War. His home became a place of worship for Methodists; a society was formed in 1812.

James Peters and his neighbors built a log house in 1814 about one hundred yards from the present church on land known as Peters' Camp Ground. Later that year a brick house of worship was erected and used until 1846, when another building was constructed.

The Spring Hill Methodist Church narrowly escaped destruction during the Civil War. According to Civil War scholars, what became the bloody Battle of Franklin might have been a Battle of Spring Hill, had General John B. Hood followed his advantage over Federal forces at the time. He did not, and the Federals slipped by and took up positions at Franklin, thus sparing the Spring Hill area.

The church building of 1846 stood until 1886, when it was razed to make way for the present one, which was erected at a cost of $5,000. The architectural style of this church is a Victorian adaptation of Gothic Revival.

Springfield Baptist Church
Springfield

The date of the organization of this church is uncertain; an early historian stated that it was founded in 1847 and later disbanded. The earliest official records stated that on March 4, 1866, representatives of Franklin and Keysburg Churches in Kentucky and Red River Church in Tennessee met, and with Elder D. Hail as presiding officer and M.V. Ingram, Secretary, Springfield Church was organized with eight members.

The Baptist congregation worshipped in the Cumberland Presbyterian church and Robertson County courthouse until their church was completed and dedicated, by Reverend W.A. Nelson, in May 1878. That brick building of Gothic design stood on Main Street near the present church. It was built by George Dalton, an early deacon, and was a one-room building.

Each church in Springfield had a bell which was rung to remind members it was time to go to church. Each bell had its own distinctive tone, telling its own members that services were beginning.

On November 30, 1913, a new church of Romanesque architecture was dedicated by J.W. Gilliam. In 1964, the present sanctuary was completed and dedicated by Pastor Grant L. Jones, followed by an organ recital by Mr. Samuel Shanko.

Springfield Baptist

Spring Hill United Methodist

First United Methodist, Springfield

First United Methodist Church Springfield

Having been an appointment in the Red River circuit for fifty years, the Methodist church in Springfield was organized soon after 1830. The site for the original building was lot number fifty-seven of the town of Springfield, and was purchased from Dr. Archibald Thomas for fifty dollars. A frame church was built there in 1837.

That first church was replaced by another frame building sometime after 1855. The sanctuary was high above ground, and a school was conducted in the basement. That building burned in 1882 and was replaced by a brick church on the same site with the entrance on Oak Street. The Kirk brothers served as architects and contractors. Henry Hart Kirk laid the brick as his gift to the church.

The cornerstone for a new church was laid in 1916; a Skinner organ was installed in 1920. The sanctuary contains several beautiful memorial windows.

First Presbyterian, Springfield

First Presbyterian Church
Springfield

This is the oldest church in Springfield. It was organized as a Cumberland Presbyterian congregation in 1837, and the first building was erected in 1839, on lot number 17 of the original plot of the town.

The first worship services were held in the Robertson County courthouse. Early in the history of this church the congregation moved from Cumberland Presbyterian affiliation to that of Presbyterian U.S.A.

During the occupation of Springfield by Union forces in the Civil War, this small church became a stable. Hoof marks are still visible on the old flooring in rooms now used for Sunday School.

The sanctuary, built in 1897 in an adaptation of Romanesque architecture, was given by Thomas Pepper in memory of his wife Mary.

New Providence Presbyterian Church
Surgoinsville

One of the oldest congregations in continuous existence west of the Allegheny Mountains, this church was organized in 1780 by Samuel Doak and Charles Cummings, who organized three other churches (Salem, Mount Bethel, and Carter's Valley) in the same year.

The original log church which stood near the present Amis Chapel Methodist Church in Carter's Valley was built about 1750 on land owned by Arthur Galbraith. Some time after 1800, New Providence moved from Carter's Valley. Hawkins County Deed Book 18 records that on "August 16, 1816, William Armstrong, Second, deeded to the Trustees of the New Providence Meeting House, a certain lot on the northeast side of Armstrong's Mill, including New Providence Meeting House and ground sufficient for a burying ground, also including the school house."

The first building on the new site was built of logs and was also used as a school; the second was built of brick; the third was a large frame building which was razed about 1866 and replaced by another frame building which burned in March, 1892. The present building was built in 1893.

In early times, the pastors of New Providence Church were also teachers in the New Providence Academy, built in 1852; it burned and was rebuilt in 1901. This building still stands, but no school has been held there since 1942.

The present church, of vernacular Gothic design, is situated atop a ridge and is reached by a long drive through a grove of trees. The drive is bordered by large boxwood shrubs. The interior features simple but handsome woodwork and the original central lighting fixture.

New Providence Presbyterian, Surgoinsville

Wilson Creek Primitive Baptist, Triune

Old Sweetwater Baptist Church
Sweetwater

This church was organized in the home of Daniel and Eunice Duggan in 1820 with sixteen charter members. It was the first church organized in the newly settled Hiwassee Purchase.

In 1821 it was decided to form two Baptist congregations, one on Fork Creek and one on Sweetwater Creek. In 1822 the Sweetwater Creek congregation became a separate church and took the name Sweetwater Baptist Church. Elder Cleveland donated land and materials for the building.

By 1846 this building had become inadequate, and a larger one was built on the same site. The oldest church in Monroe County, it is still active today.

Old Sweetwater Baptist

Wilson Creek Primitive Baptist Church
Triune

One of the earliest churches in Williamson County was Big Harpeth Baptist, organized in May 1800. The twenty charter members began at once to construct a simple log church with puncheon seats on Murfreesboro Pike three miles east of Franklin.

Garner McConnico, who was born in Lunanberg County, Virginia, came into Middle Tennessee in 1797 and organized a church. He was said to possess a religious zeal and powerful voice which, on one occasion, was heard across a roaring, rampaging river during a flood. Unable to cross over, he delivered his sermon to the congregation on the other side.

After a division among the members, a small group met on October 13, 1804, and organized Wilson Creek Primitive Church. This meeting was held in Arrington Meeting House. Their first log church was built in what is now Triune. The present brick church was erected in 1816 of simple vernacular style and was used by both Federal and Confederate troops during the Civil War. Interesting inscriptions were left by these soldiers on pews and columns, one of which is on display in the Tennessee State Museum in Nashville. The remaining columns are still in use in Wilson Creek Church.

Double Springs Church and Muster Ground
Sullivan County

Double Springs served as a muster ground during the Revolutionary War and the War of 1812. It was then known as Captain Clark's Muster Ground, since Captain Henry Clark owned the land. A Revolutionary War veteran, he served as a Washington County legislator in the North Carolina General Assembly and a justice of the peace in the first Sullivan County Court in 1780.

The muster ground was on the "Long Island Path" used by Colonel William Christian's two thousand man army on their march from Fort Patrick Henry during the Cherokee campaign in 1776. Here these men rested and drank water from the Double Springs. They were then joined by a company of men from the Watauga Settlement and proceeded to the Cherokee towns.

Near the Double Springs was built one of the earliest Baptist Churches in Tennessee. The church and nearby burial ground—one of the oldest in the state—have been in use since before 1790. Known as Kendrick Creek Church, it was founded by Jonathan Mulkey, who served as the first pastor.

The first small log church was the meeting place of the Holston Association of Baptist Churches in October 1786. The present frame building was erected in this century.

Double Springs Church

First Baptist Church
Tullahoma

The First Baptist Church in Tullahoma was organized in 1856 and worshipped in a small building on the east side of Jackson Street between Grundy and Moore Streets.

The earliest pastor named in the records is A. D. Phillips.

The present site was purchased in 1904, and in 1906 a building of concrete blocks was constructed under the direction of a German architect. It was replaced by the present handsome church, of Greek Revival architecture, in 1950.

First Baptist, Tullahoma

'irst United Methodist Church
'renton

'he church was organized in 1827 and a frame tructure, built by Thomas Fite, was completed in 834. Early records reveal that two rolls of members vere kept here—one listing names of male members nd the other listing the names of female members. Iours of services were listed as "11 A.M. to 1 or 2 ?.M."

In 1870, land was purchased and a church built; it vas the first brick building in Gibson County. Before t was completed, the congregation found the reasury empty. Instead of borrowing money to omplete it, they boarded up the windows and doors nd waited several months for enough to be raised o resume construction.

A pipe organ donated to the church by Mrs. Mary evy of Philadelphia was presented by her brother-n-law, Dr. Lewis Levy, a member of the church, and vas used for many years. A ladies' organization gave hree brass chandeliers, and many other memorials ave been placed in this Gothic Revival church.

'irst United Methodist, Trenton

First Presbyterian Church
Trenton

In October 1833, First Presbyterian Church was organized by Alexander Campbell and A. A. Grigsby. A residence on High Street was used as the first place of worship; that property was purchased in February 1836 for the site of a church, and in 1845 a frame building was erected.

Concord Presbyterian and Eaton Presbyterian churches were soon organized by the pastor and elders of the Trenton Church. A public library was organized here in 1876, and Women's Foreign Missionary Society was formed in 1886.

Money for a new sanctuary had been raised by 1889, and the Trustees were vested with authority to sell the church property and acquire a new site. On March 25, 1892, the present property was purchased. A new church was completed that same year and dedicated in early 1893.

Beautiful stained glass graces this Gothic building, which features two spires.

First Presbyterian, Trenton

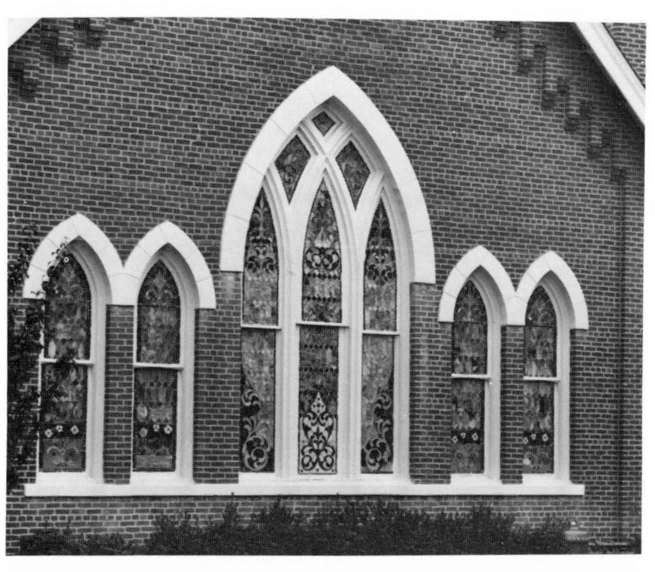

Saint James Episcopal, Union City

Saint James Episcopal Church
Union City

When General George W. Gibbs laid out the town of Union City, he gave building lots to Methodist, Baptist, Christian and Presbyterian church groups as sites for churches. Cumberland Presbyterians received no lot, since they already owned one, and none were provided for Catholics nor Episcopalians.

Mrs. Alexander Campbell, of Jackson, granddaughter of General Gibbs, gave a block on First Street as a building site for an Episcopal church, parish house, trees, shrubs, and flower garden. No church was built until much later. She was often urged to petition Bishop Thomas F. Gailor to sell the property but always refused.

In 1893, a minister named Trout arrived in Union City and was granted permission by the Waddell family to hold Episcopal worship in a little wooden building constructed and dedicated for use by the Swedenborgian Church, of which the Waddell family were members. The property on First Street was finally sold.

Dr. W.M. Turner donated another lot on First Street and the present Gothic style Saint James Episcopal Church was dedicated there in 1905.

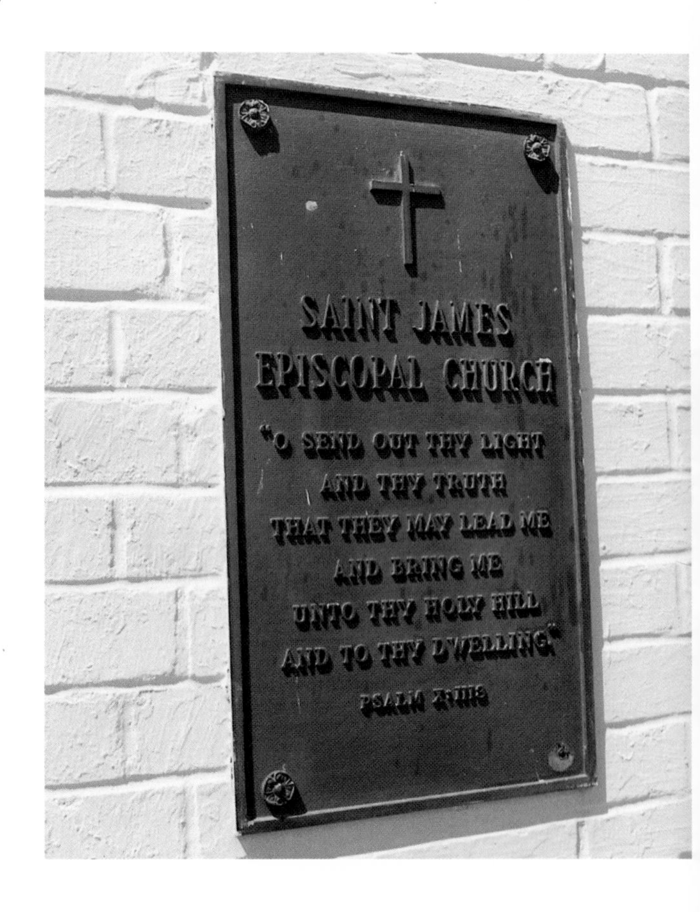

Union City Church of Christ
Union City

This church began in 1857 with fifteen members, and their first building was destroyed during the Civil War. The present church of Greco-Romanesque architecture was erected in 1949.

David Lipscomb, N. B. Hardeman, T. B. Larimore, A. G. Freed and Coleman Overby have all preached to this congregation.

Union City Church of Christ

Union City Cumberland Presbyterian Church
Union City

This church was organized in 1858 by Reverend Joe McLesky and C. W. McBride. Abandoned during the Civil War, it was reorganized in 1866 and a frame church featuring Gothic windows was built in 1867.

In 1898 a brick building was erected at the corner of Church and Home Streets. While construction was in progress, the architect, John Carter, and the builder, J. J. Dugan, both died, and Elder T. J. Harvey supervised the remainder of the work. Reverend J. A. McDonald was serving as pastor at that time.

That building burned on March 23, 1896. No records and very little furniture were saved.The present building was constructed on the old foundations by architects Tisdale, Stone and Pinson of Nashville and contractors Hill and Merryman of Fulton, Kentucky.

Union City Cumberland Presbyterian

Whitesburg Baptist Church
Whitesburg

Elders Tidence Lane and William Murphy organized this church, known as the Church of Jesus Christ, on Bent Creek and Holston Rivers, on June 12, 1785. This is the third oldest church in Tennessee.

Tidence Lane, the first pastor of Bent Creek Baptist Church and the organizer of Buffalo Ridge Baptist church near Jonesboro, is recognized as the first pastor of any church in Tennessee.

The first known worship service here was held "under the shade of a mighty elm tree, believed to have a three hundred foot spread, on the bank of Bent Creek." Later meetings were held in homes, and still later a log church was constructed near the site of the present building.

During the early years, Black members were received into the fellowship of this church, and in 1834 a Mr. Barnet, a Black man, was licensed to preach.

Bent Creek Church moved into Whitesburg in 1872 and built a two story brick house of worship, the lower floor of which was used for worship and the upper floor for meetings of the Masonic Order. This arrangement continues today in this 1872 building. The name was changed to Whitesburg Baptist Church in 1875.

Written with quill pens and dating from 1785, the minutes of this church are the oldest public records in Hamblen County.

Whitesburg Baptist

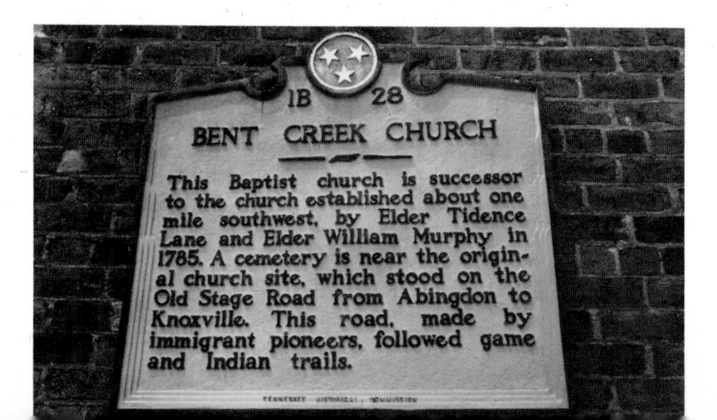

Harpeth Presbyterian Church
Williamson County

Harpeth Presbyterian Church was founded by Gideon Blackburn in 1811. The original building, built of logs, stood on grounds donated by the McCutcheon brothers, whose father had received a section of land for his service in the Revolutionary War. There were two front doors, one for Whites and one for Blacks, and the minister stood between them so that worshippers could watch for Indian and bandit attacks.

Erected in 1811, it was a sturdy building which stood until 1836, when it was torn down to make room for the present building. Mr. Robert McCutcheon and his slaves worked for six years making the kiln-dried bricks for the new church, which originally followed the same plan as the log structure.

Before the Civil War the churchyard was used as a cemetery for both White and Black people, and the surrounding area near a river ford was a camping ground for travelers. After the Battle of Nashville, Confederate soldiers took refuge from the weather in Harpeth Church.

Under the leadership of the Reverend Priesly Miller, pastor from 1948 to 1969, Harpeth Presbyterian Church experienced a revitalization of membership and the need for additional Sunday School rooms and an educational building. In 1954 a long-planned bell tower was erected and the church grounds were landscaped.

This church has been called "Little Gem on the Harpeth."

Harpeth Presbyterian, Williamson County

Goshen Cumberland Presbyterian, Winchester

**Goshen Cumberland Presbyterian Church
Winchester**

This church is the oldest in Franklin County, and is located one and one half miles southeast of the Boiling Fork of the Elk River.

Founded in 1808 by Scotch-Irish Presbyterian families, it was the first Presbyterian congregation in Tennessee to transfer to the Cumberland Presbyterian Church, whose first camp meeting was held here.

Winchester United Methodist

**Winchester United Methodist Church
Winchester**

This church was organized in 1825 and worshipped in a log building similar to Strother's Meeting House (now located on Scarritt College Campus in Nashville).

In 1834, the congregation erected a brick church three stories high. The first floor was an opera auditorium, the second floor a church sanctuary, and the third the meeting place of the Masonic Lodge. This arrangement continued for forty-one years.

The present building was erected in 1893. Bishop A. W. Wilson presided over the Tennessee Annual Conference here in 1895. Governor Peter Tuner, who was living at Hundred Oaks Castle, delivered the welcome address to the Conference.

Reverend William H. Moss, a chaplain in World War II and State Commander of the American Legion, was a former pastor of this church.

**Woodbury Church of Christ
Woodbury**

A Church of Christ congregation was organized in Woodbury in 1830. In 1836, a lot was donated by William East; a frame building was erected in 1842. Membership had grown to 100 by 1868 and 240 by 1874. The present membership is over 450.

The present simple Gothic church with two unusual octagonal towers was built in 1889; the stained glass windows are original. Additions were added in November 1951, and a portico has been added in front to protect the original doors.

In 1941, O. P. Baird became the first full-time minister. Before then, ministers had been provided on a part-time or temporary basis. Among those who had served the congregation were Tolbert Fanning, Granville Lipscomb, T. B. Larrimore, H. Leo Boles, and A. C. Pullias.

Woodbury Church of Christ

INDEX OF CHURCHES BY NAME